Secrets to a Successful

GREENHOUSE BUSINESS

T. M. Taylor

A Complete Guide to Starting and Operating
A High-Profit Business
That's Beneficial to the Environment

GreenEarth Publishing Company, Inc. ✦ P.O. Box 243 ✦ Melbourne, FL 32902

Printed in the United States of America on acid-free ∞ **,**
recycled paper ♺

If you have any questions or comments concerning this book,
please write:
 GreenEarth Publishing Company, Inc.
 Book Reader Service
 P.O. Box 243
 Melbourne, FL 32902

Book design by Sara Patton, Words of Wonder

Publisher's Cataloging in Publication
(prepared by Quality Books, Inc.)

Taylor, Ted M.
 Secrets to a Successful Greenhouse Business: A Complete Guide
 to Starting and Operating a High-Profit Business That's Beneficial to the
 Environment
Ted Michael Taylor.
 p. cm
 Includes bibliographical references and index.
 ISBN 0-9628678-0-2

 1. Greenhouse. 2. Homebased business. I. Title.
SB415   635.0483
                                          QBI91-1442

CONTENTS

Introduction

Starting a greenhouse business should be one of the most creative and satisfying endeavors you ever experience. There is nothing like the natural gratitude that comes from watching a seed or cutting grow into a large, salable plant. Building your plant nursery to the size you desire is most satisfying. The daily work produces more and more until one day, before you know it, you have what you wished for: *a profitable greenhouse business.*

With the use of automatic watering systems, timers, and other labor-saving devices, you will have plenty of time to be creative and experiment with lots of different varieties and species of unusual plants. You will also have plenty of time to seek new ways to promote your business that are not mentioned in this book. Remember: *"Find work that you love and you will never work a day in your life!"*

Start now by calling or writing some of the companies listed in Section 11 and request catalogs and credit applications. Most will approve credit for 30 days on first order.

Send for all the publications you can find. Magazines are another important tool. They are full of articles that can help you succeed in the greenhouse business and familiarize you with all phases of the business, including new products and technology that will save you time and money.

This book will reveal secrets that can mean the difference between whether you earn a little or a lot. Growing plants can be one of the most rewarding and profitable businesses you will find. After being in different high-profit projects over the last 30 years, I find that growing large quantities (10,000 or more) of the 4" to 6½" pots and selling truckload quantities at competitive prices makes this one of the best businesses in terms of profits and rewards, and it is one you can do anywhere.

Check with your state university agricultural department for new information on plant varieties of interest. Also, check with your county agricultural center or experimental station.

One of the best sources of information is a local nursery, retail, or wholesale operation. Visit as many as you can. Get their price lists for future reference. Buy some stock plants that you're interested in. Observe their watering, heating, and shading systems; this can save you a lot of time. Selling to wholesale nurseries will require a tax number that can be acquired by contacting the local Department of Revenue after you get a city license (if required) and county license.

Write down the following information for future reference: planting, spraying, fertilizing, and ready dates. This will be the beginning of your all-important nursery log.

Your county Extension Agent can provide you with information about who the active growers are, and about local growers' associations. Established growers should have informed opinions about professional contractors who install greenhouses, and about what works and what doesn't.

There are also design booklets distributed by equipment manufacturers that can be very informative. In addition, most manufacturers have technical representatives available to answer questions about design and proper installation of their equipment.

Finally, there are other Extension publications that address many topics of particular concern to the grower in greater detail than is usually found in publications intended for a national audience.

It is not important to start out with a large greenhouse (96', for example). You may want to build a portion of it now and add on later. For some people a small greenhouse business is the best way to start. By not laying out a lot of money in the beginning and by multiplying your plants, you will soon have a large, profitable operation.

You may also want to construct a shade house. This can be built like the greenhouse—just leave off the covering and put shade cloth on it. Some growers use a flat style construction which is a little cheaper.

With all the possibilities of projects—growing trees for hardwood companies and landscapers; herbs for local and grocery store chains; fruit plants and trees for homeowners, landscapers, and farmers; and foliage, annuals, pot flowers, and vegetables for all of the above and wholesale buyers and brokers, you will have no problem finding a good market for a high quality plant. At the library you can check the yellow pages of the nearest large city for brokers and other markets you are interested in, and begin getting acquainted with your potential buyers.

Section 1
Quantity and Variety

Profits, prices, quantity, and quality are key words in the greenhouse business. The time required to produce a plant that will sell and make a profit is very important. The objective is to start with proper soil and container, have a good environment for the plant to grow, then market the plant in the most profitable way.

Growing a large assortment is nice if you have the room and the time to care for them. For fast profits, grow large single crops. Specialty items will bring bigger and faster rewards. Growing ten varieties with different watering, spraying, fertilizer, and shade requirements; then getting them ready at different times and performing the dozens of different sales and deliveries that have to be made can result in a loss of profit and time. You can grow 10,000 of one type of plant as easily as 2,000 of assorted varieties with less time and trouble.

With large quantities of a few varieties of plants, you can get the attention of big buyers who purchase large quantities on a regular basis. These buyers demand healthy, clean, marketable plants. Show them you can supply this and they will keep you sold out months in advance. These will be general orders that

amount to between $1,000 and $10,000 per order. Large promotion orders of 300 to 500 boxes containing 12 pots per box (6" size) would be a truckload quantity, ranging from $5,000 to $10,000 and up. These plants can be delivered by you (the way to start), or you can have the buyer pay a freight line to pick them up. The biggest concern at this point should be quality control. Make sure all plants are inspected and packed properly. The care taken at this point will ensure repeat orders.

In choosing what to grow to obtain good profits, you must select the right combination of profitable plant varieties, sizes, and quantities. After determining your technical ability to grow plants of acceptable quality, decide which plants can be most profitably produced by:

1. Estimating plant production costs;

2. Comparing expected market prices of individual plants with estimated production costs;

3. Comparing expected net returns among plant varieties and sizes on a common basis.

Often growers base pricing upon competitors' prices. Both market price and production costs must be considered. Knowledge of actual production costs of individual plants helps you make plant selection decisions based on profits.

BESTSELLERS

Annuals, herbs, and foliage are your best-selling plants. All had outstanding sales in 1989 and 1990. Foliage increased a little and herbs did the best with a 25% increase in sales. There are not enough growers to give this county anywhere near a saturation point. I predict that herb sales will increase 100% in the next couple of years, and will never stop increasing. More people are watching what they eat, and herbs take the place of artificial flavors, salt, and stimulants. If possible, grow them organically.

PLANT SALES

Over 50% of the growers who responded to a survey said 1991 was their best year yet for annuals.

Impatiens were overwhelmingly named the bestselling bedding plant, except in the west where grandiflora petunias ranked highest. Those surveyed ranked grandiflora petunias as the second bestseller overall, followed by cutting geraniums. Vinca was mentioned as a bestseller in the south.

The predominant wholesale price range per flat is $8.00; the retail price range is around $10.00. The most popular flat size is the 48, followed by the 72-unit tray. The same report indicated that 4" production has jumped again.

Two-thirds of respondents expect their overall bedding plant production to increase. Impatiens, cutting geraniums, seed geraniums, and French marigolds are expected to be the leaders.

The Professional Plant Growers Association has published a 1990-91 catalog of educational material and products designed for the commercial grower. Included are PPGA's videos, "Blooming Profits; Merchandising Plants for the Garden" and "Safe Handling of Pesticides"; also safety signs and labels for pesticide storage areas and controlled temperature areas, and bedding plant information (for retailers). The catalog is also full of references to books covering subjects from finance to greenhouse operation, production methods, management, perennials, geraniums, bulbs, as well as the third edition of PPGA's Grower Guide reference collection of extension and university bulletins.

Professional Plant Growers Association, the international trade association for the greenhouse industry (originally Bedding Plants, Inc.) serves growers of all greenhouse crops and members of related industries. You may request a free copy of the catalog, along with membership information, from PPGA, P.O. Box 27517, Lansing, MI, 48909, (517) 694-7700.

BEDDING PLANTS - FLOWERING POT PLANTS

All plants that grow to maturity in less than one year and then die are called annuals. Plants that live through more than one growing season from dormant tissue are called perennials.

Bedding plants come from both of these groups. Being one of the largest segments of the plant business, some attention should be given to them. Just about all areas of the country, from rural farming areas to populated cities, can use dozens more growers. The key is to visit area nurseries, talk with local and out-of-town buyers, and pick a few varieties that will have no competition. Try to start a growing plan that will involve seeding flats of individual packs and 4" pots on weekly intervals. The following plants are some of the basic bestsellers, but new hybrids of lasting color can be the ticket you need.

Asters	Gerber Daisy	Snapdragons
Begonias	Herbs	Tomatoes
Black-Eyed Susans	Impatiens	Peppers
Chrysanthemums	Marigolds	Periwinkle
Coleus	Petunias	Cucumbers
Dianthus	Portulaca	Thunbergia
Geranium	Roses	Zinnias

With most varieties, seeding more than one seed and then picking out extras after plants are 1" high is the best method. Water containing a high salt level should not be used. Liquid feed of a water-soluble fertilizer like Peters 20-20-20 is the all-around best.

After selecting your major crops, contact your local agriculture experimental station for the latest information on growing procedures and fertilizer requirements.

You may want to use growth regulators on some types to slow growth or give plants a more compact look. Check with your local supplier for availability. B-Nine and A-Rest are the most popular.

The biggest profit will be achieved with plants that you can produce by plantlets, cuttings, or seeds in which you may use stock plants. For instance, an overgrown golden pathos hanging basket with 20 or so runners will make 300 to 400 starts or cuttings. Putting 3 or 4 cuttings (which is common practice) in each 4" pot, you can make 100 pots and still have the mother plant. Spider plants are also easily propagated by pulling the plantlet once little roots have appeared, and sticking it 1" into the soil.

ANNUALS

It is possible to have color for sale during all seasons of the year. This can be accomplished by selecting annual flowering plants for each season. Some will thrive during the hot summer months, while others grow well during the cool part of the year. By carefully selecting these annuals, you can have color all year round. The following list will help you select these annuals.

NAME	WHEN TO SOW SEED	APPROXIMATE TIME IN BLOOM	TENDER OR HARDY
Ageratum (Floss flower)	Feb. - April	May - August	Tender
Alyssum	Sept. - Jan.	Oct. - June	Hardy
Arctotis (African daisy)	Aug. - Jan.	Mar. - June	Hardy
Aster	Feb. - April	June - Aug.	Tender
Balsam	Feb. - April	April - Sept.	Tender

continued

NAME	WHEN TO SOW SEED	APPROXIMATE TIME IN BLOOM	TENDER OR HARDY
Calendula	Sept. - Jan.	Dec. - May	Hardy
Calliopsis	Oct. - May	April - June	Hardy
Celosia (Cockscomb)	Feb. - April	May - Sept.	Tender
Chrysanthemum (annual)	Feb. - March	May- July	Tender
Cleome	Sept. - May	April - Aug.	Hardy
Cornflower (Bachelor's buttons)	Sept. - Jan.	Dec. - June	Hardy
Cosmos	Feb. - April	May - Aug.	Tender
Cypress Vine	March - May	July - Sept.	Tender
Dahlia	March - April	May - Sept.	Tender
Delphinium	Sept. - Nov.	March - May	Hardy
Dianthus (pinks)	Sept. March	Nov. - June	Hardy
Four O'Clock	Feb. - May	April - Sept.	Tender
Gaillardia (Blanket flower)	Sept. - Jan.	April - Aug.	Hardy
Gomphrena (Globe amaranth)	March - April	May-July	Tender
Gypsophila (Baby's breath)	Sept. - Dec.	Oct. - June	Tender
Gourd	Feb. - April		Tender
Hollyhock	Sept. - Dec.	March - June	Hardy
Helichrysum (Strawflower)	March - May	May - Aug.	Tender
Ipomea (Morning glory)	Feb. - April	March - Nov.	Tender
Larkspur	Oct. - Dec.	March - May	Hardy
Lobelia	Sept. - March	Nov. - May	Tender
Lupine	Sept. - Dec.	Feb. - April	Hardy
Marigold	Feb. - May	May - Nov.	Tender
Nasturtium	Feb. - March	April - June	Tender
Pansy	Sept. - Dec.	June - May	Hardy
Petunia	Aug. - Jan.	Jan. - July	Hardy

continued

NAME	WHEN TO SOW SEED	APPROXIMATE TIME IN BLOOM	TENDER OR HARDY
Phlox	Sept. - Feb.	Dec. - May	Hardy
Poppy	Nov. - Jan.	March - May	Hardy
Portulaca (Rose moss)	Feb. - May	May- Sept.	Tender
Salvia (red sage)	Feb. - May	April - Sept.	Tender
Salvia (blue)	Sept. - June	March - Sept.	Hardy
Snapdragon	Sept. - Dec.	Feb. - June	Hardy
Statice	Sept. - Dec.	Feb. - Aug.	Hardy
Sweet Pea	Oct. - Jan.	Jan. - April	Hardy
Torenia	March - Sept.	May - Nov.	Tender
Verbena	Sept. - Dec.	Feb. - July	Hardy
Zinnia	Feb. - Aug.	April - Oct.	Tender

FOR CUT FLOWERS

Aster	Calendula	Calliopsis	Celosia
Chrysanthemum	Cornflower	Cosmos	Dahlia
Delphinium	Dianthus	Gaillardia	Gomphrena
Gypsophila	Helichrysum	Larkspur	Lupine
Marigold	Phlox	Poppy	Salvia
Snapdragon	Statice	Sweet Pea	Zinnia

FOR BORDERS

Ageratum	Alyssum	Lobelia	Marigold (dwarf)
Nasturtium	Pansy	Portulaca	Zinnia (dwarf)

SUMMER ANNUALS
(PLANT IN SPRING)

Balsam	Calliopsis	Celosia	Chrysanthemum
Cypress Vine	Dahlia	Four O'Clock	Gaillardia
Ipomea	Marigold	Portulaca	Tithonia
Torenia	Salvia	Zinnia	

PLUG FLATS

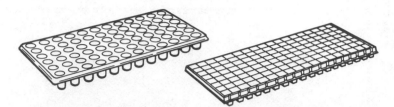

SIZE	QTY./CS.	DIMENSIONS		PRICE PER CASE		
		TOP	DEPTH	1-9	10-24	25-UP
24 Round	100	2-3/8'' Rd.	2-5/16''	$44.70	$42.45	$40.30
38 Round	100	2-3/16'' Rd.	2-5/16''	44.70	42.45	40.30
50 Round	100	1-7/8'' Rd.	2-5/16''	44.70	42.45	40.30
72 Round	100	1-1/2'' Rd.	2-5/16''	44.70	42.45	40.30
98 Round	100	1-3/8'' Rd.	1-1/2''	44.70	42.45	40.30
162 Round	100	1'' Rd.	1-1/2''	44.70	42.45	40.30
288 Round	100	13/16'' Rd.	1''	44.70	42.45	40.30
50 Square	100	1-3/4'' Sq.	2-1/4''	48.40	45.95	43.65
72 Square	100	1-9/16'' Sq.	2-3/16''	48.40	45.95	43.65
128 Square	100	1-3/16'' Sq.	1-3/16''	48.40	45.95	43.65
162 Square	100	1-1/16'' Sq.	1-1/2''	48.40	45.95	43.65
200 Square	100	15/16'' Sq.	1-1/2''	48.40	45.95	43.65
406 Square	100	5/8'' Sq.	7/8''	48.40	45.95	43.65

BEDDING PLANT CONTAINERS

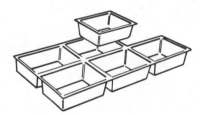

601
1 compartment per pack
Six packs per flat
Pack size: 7'' x 5-1/4'' x 2-5/16''
600 packs (100 sheets) per carton

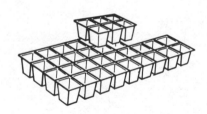

606
6 compartments per pack
Six packs per flat
Pack Size: 7'' x 5-1/4'' x 2-5/16''
600 packs (100 sheets) per carton

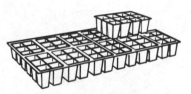

612
12 compartments per pack
Six packs per flat
Pack Size: 7'' x 5-1/4'' x 2-5/16''
600 packs (100 sheets) per carton

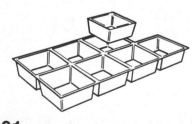

801
1 compartment per pack
Eight packs per flat
Pack Size: 5-1/4'' x 5-1/4'' x 2-5/16''
800 packs (100 sheets) per carton

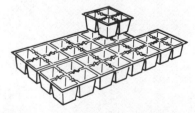

804
4 compartments per pack
Eight packs per flat
Pack Size: 5-1/4'' x 5-1/4'' x 2-5/16''
800 packs (100 sheets) per carton

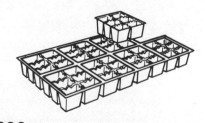

806
6 compartments per pack
Eight packs per flat
Pack Size: 5-1/4'' x 5-1/4'' x 2-5/16''
800 packs (100 sheets) per carton

BEDDING PLANT CONTAINERS

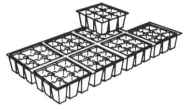

809
9 compartments per pack
Eight packs per flat
Pack Size: 5-1/4'' x 5-1/4'' x 2-5/16''
800 packs (100 sheets) per carton

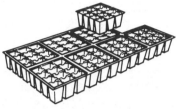

812
12 compartments per pack
Eight packs per flat
Pack Size: 5-1/4'' x 5-1/4'' x 2-5/16''
800 packs (100 sheets) per carton

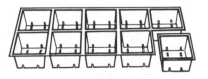

1001
10 packs per sheet, 1 cell per pack

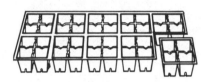

1004
10 packs per sheet, 4 cells per pack

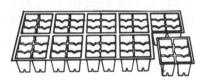

1006
10 packs per sheet, 6 cells per pack

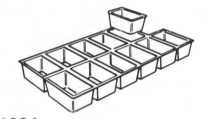

1201
1 compartment per pack
Twelve packs per flat
Pack Size: 3-1/2'' x 5-1/4'' x 2-5/16''
1200 packs (100 sheets) per carton

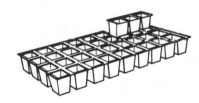

1203
3 compartments per pack
Twelve packs per flat
Pack Size: 7'' x 2-3/8'' x 2-5/16''
1200 packs (100 sheets) per carton

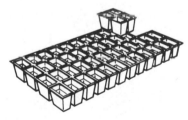

1204
4 compartments per pack
Twelve packs per flat
Pack Size: 3-1/2'' x 5-1/4'' x 2-5/16''
1200 packs (100 sheets) per carton

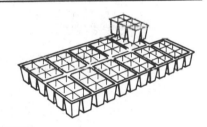

1206
6 compartments per pack
Twelve packs per flat
Pack Size: 3-1/2'' x 5-1/4'' x 2-5/16''
1200 packs (100 sheets) per carton

TRAYS

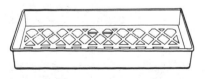

Description		Price/Bdl.
Medium wt. 1020 flat,	1-9	$21.50
50/bdl. (open bottom,	10-47	18.30
solid sides)	48 & Up	17.20

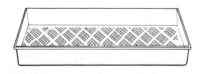

Description		Price/Bdl.
Heavy wt. 1020 flat,	1-9	$25.00
50/bdl. (solid bottom	10-47	21.25
and sides w/drainage)	48 & Up	20.00

CONTAINERS

Plastic Pots

DESCRIPTION	QTY/CS.	1-9 CS.	PER M	10-24 CS.	PER M	25-UP CS.	PER M
3" Square	1400	$38.77	$ 27.70	$36.00	$ 25.70	$33.60	$ 24.00
3" Round	1200	51.69	43.10	48.00	40.00	44.80	37.30
3-1/2" Round	1200	57.23	47.70	53.14	44.30	49.60	41.30
4" Geranium	900	47.08	52.30	43.71	48.60	40.80	45.30
4-1/2" Geranium	900	52.62	58.50	48.86	54.30	45.60	50.70
4" Azalea	1000	47.69	47.69	44.29	44.29	41.33	41.33
5" Azalea	600	50.77	84.60	47.14	78.60	44.00	73.30
6" Standard	300	42.00	140.00	39.00	130.00	36.40	121.30
6" Azalea	300	29.77	99.20	27.64	92.10	25.80	86.00
6-1/2" Azalea	300	38.10	127.00	36.60	122.00	32.90	109.70
7" Azalea	300	66.92	223.10	62.14	207.10	58.00	193.30
7-1/2" Azalea	300	71.54	238.50	66.43	221.40	62.00	206.70
8" Azalea	240	98.00	408.30	94.10	392.10	90.30	376.30

DIA. X HGT.	QTY./ BNDL.	1-24 BNDL.	25-49 BNDL.	50-UP BNDL.
4-3/4" x 4-3/4"	150	$19.03	$17.90	$16.89
6-1/4" x 6"	125	18.06	16.99	16.03
6-3/4" x 6-1/2"	100	15.68	14.75	13.92
6-3/4" x 7-1/4"	125	21.54	20.25	19.11
8" x 5"	125	21.79	20.49	19.34
7-3/4" x 7"	75	18.33	17.24	16.27
8" x 8-1/2"	100	30.13	28.33	26.73
9" x 6"	100	24.25	22.81	21.52
8-3/4" x 8-1/2"	100	31.89	29.99	28.30
10" x 9"	75	29.41	27.66	26.10
11" x 9-1/2"	50	22.38	21.05	19.86
12" x 11"	50	42.25	39.73	37.49

Hanging Baskets with Wire Hangers

DESCRIPTION	QTY/CS.	1-9 CS.	PER M	10-24 CS.	PER M	25-UP CS.	PER M
6" Green	50	$23.53	$ 470.60	$22.54	$ 450.80	$21.33	$ 426.60
6" White	50	23.53	470.60	22.54	450.80	21.33	426.60
8" Green	50	25.39	507.80	24.27	485.40	23.24	464.80
8" White	50	25.39	507.80	24.27	485.40	23.24	464.80
8" Floral Green	50	25.39	507.80	24.27	485.40	23.24	464.80
8" Floral White	50	25.39	507.80	24.27	485.40	23.24	464.80
8" Floral Green	50	25.39	507.80	24.27	485.40	23.24	464.80
8" Floral White	50	25.39	507.80	24.27	485.40	23.24	464.80
10" Green	25	17.92	716.80	16.80	672.00	15.81	632.40
10" White	25	17.92	716.80	16.80	672.00	15.81	632.40
12" Green	25	40.39	1615.60	38.60	1544.00	36.97	1478.80
12" White	25	40.39	1615.60	38.60	1544.00	36.97	1478.80

SOWING SEEDS

Seeds may be sown in boxes, pots, or outdoors. If using some sort of container, make sure that drainage will not be a problem. Seeds may be sown in vermiculite, peat moss, sand, or a mixture of these.

Outdoor seed beds should have several inches of some organic material such as peat moss added and mixed in. At the same time, mix in 1 to 1½ pounds of a 1-1-1 ratio complete fertilizer for each 10 cubic feet of soil.

A coffee cup holds about ½ pound of a complete fertilizer; a one-pound coffee can holds about 2 pounds.

Seeds may be sown in pots or broadcast in trays. An inexperienced grower should sow the seeds in pots. This is ideal for slow-germinating seeds, since fast-growing weeds may be recognized easily and removed without disturbing the germinating seeds. Weeds starting near the seed may be removed as soon as they appear.

Seed germination will depend on the temperature, moisture, and oxygen. Thus, a seed bed in a shaded area would be desirable; otherwise, the hot sun will injure or kill the young seedlings as they develop. Well-drained soil will ensure good oxygen content, which is one of the requirements of plant growth. The soil should be moist, but not allowed to get too wet or remain that way for any length of time. Good air circulation through the seed bed is also important, as it helps prevent damping off.

Depth of sowing will depend on size of seed. A general rule is to sow seeds to a depth of about three to four times their diameter. Small seeds are sprinkled on the ground surface and pressed into place.

Young seedlings should be transplanted as soon as they are large enough to handle. This tends to harden the plant, making it more able to withstand adverse weather conditions.

FOLIAGE PLANTS

Most foliage plants come originally from the tropical forest regions and the temperate cooler climates. Those foliage plants native to tropical forests are grown under the shade of trees (the light level being 63% to 73% shade), in hot temperatures and high humidity. Find out the shade requirements of the particular type of plants you will be growing from your local county extension office. Most foliage will do nicely with 73% shade in summer and 55% or less in winter. Herbs, annuals, and some nursery stock grow better under light shade in summer. Use a light meter which measures foot candles, usually on a scale of 1 to 10. These units are inexpensive and come with a user's guide. Become aware of light levels on cloudy days, winter, summer, and fall. Check throughout your greenhouse to see if any areas are affected by overhead obstacles.

For some rare types of plants you may want to artificially shade plants to inspire flowering. Again, check with your county extension experimental station for the latest information on the type you're growing.

High pressure sodium and metal halide lamps may be used to get faster growth and to extend daylight hours when starting seeds. Try this when you are able for some astounding results in winter. Bottom heating pads are also recommended for fast results starting cuttings or seeds in weather below 65°.

Pothos and spider plants are very simple for beginners to grow and are in high demand almost everywhere. These plants seem to tolerate wide changes in soil mixture, fertilizer, light, water, and temperature without serious loss of quality. They are also immune to most serious diseases and insects. I suggest starting these in 500 to 1500 4" pots while planning your greenhouse business. The practice and experience—

and just getting started—is important while you are researching other crops and building your greenhouse. A large quantity of foliage can be grown under shade trees or on the east side close to your house or apartment.

To grow foliage plants you need a soil that will hold lots of moisture, 18-6-12 fertilizer slow release, and 4 hours of morning sunlight or 50% to 75% shade cloth. You will get much faster results with a greenhouse where you can raise the humidity and at the same time lower the temperature with fans at one end pulling air through the other end. Using white paint on double poly greenhouses achieves more shade without the use of shade cloth.

Foliage plants are the fastest growing type of plant and require lots of good water. The first step in starting a plant nursery is to take two samples to your county extension office, who will test for soluble salts at no charge! This level should not be over 700 ppm—the lower the better. Deep wells near the ocean might be too salty, while a shallow well in the same locaton will be acceptable. Ponds, lakes, and rivers are excellent water sources.

Now that you have a good water supply, make sure when planting cuttings, plantlets, or seeds that the soil is wet all the way through, and never let them completely dry out or growth will stop. Fill pots with soil and fertilizer, then water once before planting.

Filling 500 4" pots requires about 9 cubic feet of potting soil, purchased locally at wholesale growers supply companies for about $7.00 per 3-cubic-foot bag. Peat moss is a great soil additive that is discussed in Section 7. It can be mixed with any type of potting mix to enhance water-holding capabilities.

When planting cuttings, a root hormone powder can be used to speed rooting, but is not necessary on most foliage plants. Make sure the water drains slowly all the way through the pot to get good coverage.

Some philodendrons and bushy foliage plants will need some fungicide and insecticide spraying about every seven to ten days (see Section 6). Lowering the humidity slightly will usually eliminate most fungus.

A discussion of all foliage plant varieties can be found in the *Exotic Plant Manual and Tropical* by A. B. Graf. This book is the growers' bible in the foliage plant industry.

Some of the families of foliage plants that you will need to know are:

Aroid – philodendron, pothos, anthurium, diffenbachia, syngonium, algaonemas, spathiphylem

Lily – dracena, asparagus sprengeri, chlorophytum, succulents, cordy line

Palm – areca, parlor, neanthe belle

Fig – ficus benjamina, rubber trees

Peperomia – many types, wandering jews

Ferns – Boston, tree, staghorn, sword

Mint – coleus, swedish ivy

Aralia – schefflera, aralias, inies

GROW FERNS FOR RELIABLE SALES

At least 63% to 70% shade is required for ferns. Measured levels should be between 1100 and 1800 foot candles. This can also be estimated by looking at the shadow cast by your hand on a bench top. If the shadow is visible but the outline is not really sharp, then the light level is okay.

Fastest fern growth occurs around 78°, so the high should be kept below 85°. Night temperatures can dip to 55 or 50° without hurting most ferns, with the exception of curly bird's nest and some of the less common ferns such as knightae, solida, and feejensis. We recommend a low of 62 to 65° for commercial production.

Ferns do not like to stay "dripping wet." Some of them actually like to lightly dry out between waterings: all of the footed ferns, the bird's nest ferns, and the Boston family. Others that will wilt if they dry out include tree ferns, button ferns, and maidenhair ferns. Misting ferns really doesn't have any value.

Because of the need to grow ferns in a mix that drains well, and because most ferns do not store nutrients, it is best to keep them on continuous feed. A good starting point is 100 parts per million nitrogen (using a balanced 20-20-20 or a 4:1:3 ratio if mixing your own). This rate can be increased if the foliage is too light green in color, indicating a need for increased nitrogen. The ammonia and nitrate nitrogen levels should be approximately equal.

All chemicals used to control pests can cause damage to ferns. Each must be tested carefully on a small block and then used only as needed. Repeated use, especially of fungicides, can cause problems. The generally safe chemicals are the wettable powder forms of Diazinon and Benlate. Cygon 2E is a safe drench and Mavrik is good for aphid control.

Ferns prefer a mix that has a high proportion of organic materials such as peat, and one that drains very well. The pH of the mix should be around 6.0, and there should be a source of calcium and magnesium included. Superphosphate can be left out for most ferns. Some potassium mintrate (½ pound per yard) helps ferns get started.

pH: The secret to growing those stubborn varieties of ferns is to keep the irrigating water pH between 5.8 and 6.2. This will allow you to grow beautiful giant staghorn ferns that are otherwise very difficult to grow.

PLUGS

Plugs, liners, and seedlings purchased from wholesale growers and potted (usually in a 6" pot or larger) can be finished and ready for delivery in two to four weeks. These starter plants are usually very healthy and disease-free, and sometimes come in reusable seedling trays. Addresses of growers who sell these plants are listed in Section 11. New varieties are coming out regularly. Once you order some your supplier will keep you informed of when and how to plant what.

Acquiring Stock: One of the fastest and most profitable ways to build up inventory is to mass-produce cuttings or plantlets from stock. Purchase only the most healthy overgrown plants from your local plant nursery or have them shipped to you from a large commercial wholesaler.

Tissue culture plugs are the best to start with if you have the time. They are available in all the most popular types such as poinsettias, philodendron, ferns, violets, and many more.

By taking cuttings regularly and planting them, you will soon have any amount of stock you desire. Many businesses and homeowners will give you all the landscaping cuttings you need if you offer to give them a free pruning job. Save all uprooted plants when installing new landscaping to old landscaped areas. Plant in an out-of-the-way area for future stock cuttings.

Large growers regularly throw away cuttings from prunings, and several times a year they toss leftovers from large orders with the pots still attached. Having a friend who works for one of these growers can be a valuable asset.

The main objective is to produce the most profit from a limited space as quickly as possible. Foliage plants are sold in every size imaginable. The best, most popular sellers are 4", 6", 8", and 10" pots and hanging baskets.

The 4" size usually only takes a few weeks to root or grow from seed. This is the size that most growers start with and should become your best, most profitable seller. The 4" pot sells for $1.00 to $3.00. The 8" hanging baskets sell for $2.50 to $10.00 each, with a few higher-priced varieties. The 10" or 3-gallon pots bring from $4.00 to $15.00, again depending on the variety of plant. These sizes are my most profitable. They can also bring in higher prices due to their leaf size and age of the plant. Section 8 presents a more complete price guide.

TISSUE CULTURE

Tissue culture is the best way to grow foliage plants. It is usually the most costly method, but you are guaranteed a disease-free plant.

The process of growing cells of plants in test tubes, then multiplying them by the thousands, is known as tissue cultures. Cells of plant material are sterilely put in large test tubes or jars on a sterile agar medium consisting of growth hormones, organic and inorganic chemicals, agar, and sucrose. Usually a bud or leaf section is placed in the medium, then placed under consistent light cycle and temperature (usually a 12- to 16-hour light cycle and around 77° constant).

A good book on tissue culture is *Plants from Test Tubes* by Lydiane Ryte. You can grow over one million plants from one start in less than a year by dividing the culture every three weeks. After the appropriate size plantlet is reached it is transferred from the sterile growth chamber to sterile potting soil and kept moist until normal growth persists.

Tissue cultures are usually used to clone plants that are extremely healthy and disease-resistant, since the cultured plant will be identical to the mother plant. They are also used to grow ferns that are slow to start from spores are not consistent in size to separate from clumps.

Some of the most popular tissue culture liners are Boston fern, orchids, Gerber daisies, chrysanthemums, rhododendron, and many tropical foliage plants.

ORGANICALLY GROWN HERBS

Among the heartiest and most useful houseplants are several varieties of herbs that can be used for culinary purposes. Herbs provide an interesting array of greenery, leaf texture, and form when used as houseplants. They give character and new aromas to your cooking. Indoor herb plants give the promise of spring during the winter. The ten best herbs to grow for indoor plants (and also outside gardens) are: dwarf basil, chives, chervil, dill (bouquet), oregano, parsley, sage, summer savory, sweet marjoram, and thyme.

Start these in 4" pots. Seeds are planted so that multiple plants will exist. Cover and water daily, with organic fertilizer if possible. Fish emulsion or seaweed extract are probably the best; earthworm casings also work really well when mixed in with potting soil.

Spraying herbs with any product not safe for humans to eat should not be done. Safer® brand is preferred on herbs (and on all plants). Pyrethrum spray mix can be made easily at home and is my favorite! Mix 2 tablespoons of freshly ground dried pyrethrum flowers with 1 gallon of hot water, then add a little soft soap. Let mixture stand 20 minutes before using. This will not harm fish, waterfowl, plants, or animals. Nichols Herb and Rare Seeds at 1190 North Pacific Hwy, Albany, OR, 97321 has 100% pyrethrum powder in 5-lb. boxes and has a high .9% active ingredient. It can be used as a dust also, and has a shelf life of approximately 2 to 3 years.

Local department stores (K-Mart, Walmart, etc.) readily buy herbs from vendors out of their truck or van. To get a vendor number (you need this to do business with most department stores), see the store manager. He will get you an application to sell. In a few weeks you will receive a vendor number from the head office. Try to get all payments in cash, especially from the big chains.

Another profitable way is to start seeds in a tray called the "Speedling Seedling Tray" from Speedling Inc., Sun City, Florida. This tray is made of styrofoam with 200 1"-square inverted pyramids. Seeds are started in a peat moss and vermiculite mixture and easily transplanted into pots or hanging baskets. Try putting four or five in a 8" or 10" hanging basket. These will sell on sight!

Try to grow as many varieties as possible. Be sure to contact all local groceries, nurseries, and health food stores. If they are not familiar with selling herbs, one approach is to leave a few of each variety for a week, then return for your order. A good herb book that you can leave with the manager for a couple of weeks is another great idea.

GROW HERBS FOR SCHOOLS

Grow herbs for schools and colleges. Growing 1000 4" pots, then arranging these into a designed herb garden, is very profitable. Contact your local college's horticultural department, high schools, garden clubs, and city parks. In your proposal include ground preparation, fertilizing, watering, care instructions, and a short maintenance period. Prices are usually twice the retail price, which will allow for soil additives, fertilizer, planting, and a couple of months' maintenance.

Be sure to use Safer® brand insect sprays and instruct the appropriate personnel on the upkeep, use, and growing habits of each herb. This project gives you great public relations and community service exposure.

Parsley, chives, and oregano grown for harvesting are really good moneymakers. All restaurants use large amounts of parsley. Chives and oregano are used by most exclusive restaurants. To get started selling them, take a few bunches of each (usually packed into one-pound packages) and give them to the head chef. Stress that you can make fast deliveries when needed. Fresh chives and basil will sell themselves. Prices vary from area to area, but all are very profitable.

EDIBLE FLOWERS

Alyssum   *Mustard*
Borage   *Nasturtiums*
Cilantro   *Pansy*
Geraniums   *Pineapple Sage*
Lemon Gem   *Squash*
Marigold   *Yellow Bok Choy*
Lime   *Violets*

These plants produce colorful, flavorful blooms. There are many restaurants that now purchase them when they can get them. (Even the Holiday Inns here in Florida use them.) They are a real attention-getter and the restaurants know it. Use only non-toxic sprays for insects and diseases. Packaged in small clear plastic boxes (acquired from local box company), these can be sold by the count or ounce. Prices vary greatly from area to area. Call the nearest grower of these and get his price list, then start a few cents cheaper at first. Quite a few bars will buy borage and other blooms for mixed drinks.

GROWING VEGGIES

Produce can be a most profitable item to grow. The time of year will determine your profits. Grow either squash (yellow or zucchini), peppers, burpless cucumbers, or tomatoes. These bring the best prices in the winter months (January and February), and harvest at $50.00 per bushel. A large profit can easily be made in less than 45 days with hardly any fertilizer or special knowledge in the growing field.

All special questions pertaining to bugs and fertilizer can be answered by contacting the plant doctor at the experimental station in your area. The stations are constantly experimenting with different fertilizers and growing techniques to see which are most suitable to the various areas of farming, whether it is food products or foliage plants. We have occasionally supplied them with plant material which they plant under a number of different situations. They record their reports and findings in booklets that are easily obtained just by asking. Be sure you thoroughly research the varieties you choose. This will save you time and money. Find out which are the best plants to grow for top quality in your area. This information can be found by getting opinions from a local nursery.

Prices are ighest in January, February, March, and April, so plan for your crops to be ready to harvest then if possible. Squash prices range from $20 to $50 per bushel during the winter. Bell peppers bring approximately $20 to $30 per bushel. Burpless cukes are sold by the count, usually around 50¢ each. Tomatoes vary greatly, depending on the Mexican and Florida crops. The price can be $10 to $30 per 25-pound box. Yellow tomatoes are a very good item to grow for all markets, and bring approximately 30% more profit. They have a less acid taste and are delicious. Fresh vegetables, except tomatoes, are usually packed in a wooden bushel box. Tomatoes are packed in cardboard boxes that hold 25 pounds. Check your local markets for grade information before growing.

There are three good ways to sell tomatoes: (1) groceries, (2) brokers, and (3) roadside stands. The most profitable is a roadside stand. You can realize about twice as much as when selling to a broker. Also, a roadside stand is a good sound business that could fit in with your nursery easily. Plants, gourds, and crafts can also be sold at roadside stands. Another alternate to selling is to contact a broker. They can usually be found at the farmer's market or in the yellow pages of your local directory. You will have to deliver your product to him, usually very early in the morning. The benefit here is that you can sell many bushels at one time. However, you will get approximately 20% less than the current wholesale market price. Contact local restaurants, grocery stores, and roadside stands to find out the going market price.

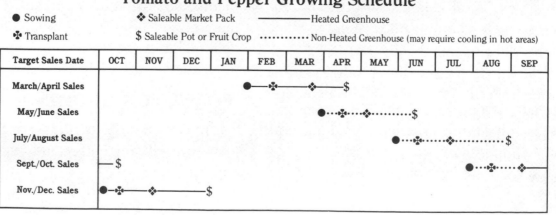

Tomato and Pepper Growing Schedule

● Sowing ❖ Saleable Market Pack ——— Heated Greenhouse
✣ Transplant $ Saleable Pot or Fruit Crop ·········· Non-Heated Greenhouse (may require cooling in hot areas)

Target Sales Date	OCT	NOV	DEC	JAN	FEB	MAR	APR	MAY	JUN	JUL	AUG	SEP
March/April Sales					●—✣——	—❖—	—$					
May/June Sales						●···✣···❖·······$						
July/August Sales								●··✣····❖·······$				
Sept./Oct. Sales	—$										●··✣····❖	
Nov./Dec. Sales	●·✣—	—❖—	—$									

Section 2
Specialized Projects with Excellent Profit Potential

HYDROPONIC VEGETABLES

Tomatoes and burpless cucumbers are the most profitable vegetables to grow. Seedling plants are started in rockwool blocks 4" wide, then transplanted to slabs that usually run the length of the greenhouse. Rows are about 4' apart. Plants are watered with a balanced mixture for each type, pumped from a fiberglass tank (or concrete). A 100' greenhouse requires a tank that holds approximately 500 gallons. Drip emitters are placed at each plant and turned on with an automatic timer. Nutrients are not allowed to overfill rockwool, so there is no runoff. There are lots of books on the subject of complete vegetable care. Read a couple of them to get good technical information.

Major grocery stores are always looking for hydroponic tomatoes in the winter and burpless cucumbers all year round.

Telephone the produce buyer for the store of your choice. Tell him who and where you are. Ask if he would be interested in seeing your vegetables, and invite him out or take a box of samples to him. Promotional videotapes come in handy here.

EXACTLY WHAT IS ROCKWOOL?

As Hawaiian legend goes, rockwool was first produced by Pele, the goddess of volcanoes. In ancient Hawaii, molten lava from erupting volcanoes left a trail of threads as it passed over natural steam vents in the ground below it. Hawaiians called this fiber "Pele's hair."

Today's rockwool for the horticulture industry is either produced from rock alone, or from a combination of rock, limestone, and coke. The components are melted at temperatures exceeding 2,500°F. This molten solution is poured over a spinning cylinder. As the molten solution flies off the cylinder, it elongates and cools to form fibers. The resultant fibers, rockwool, are then pressed into sheets, cubes, or blocks, or are granulated.

FORMS FOR GROWING

Rockwool is available in growing slabs, growing blocks, or granulated form. Slabs are rectangular pieces of rockwool which form the foundation for most of the rockwool systems in Europe. They are designed for long-term crops such as greenhouse-grown vegetables and cut flowers. Slabs may be laid directly on the ground or placed on polyethylene plastic. Rockwool blocks containing plants are set on top of slabs. Roots grow through the block and into the slabs. A nutrient solution may be applied through a spray or drip emitter, either directly to the slab or through the growing block.

Blocks are commonly used for germinating seed or rooting cuttings. The vertically oriented fibers in blocks promote good downward root growth.

Granulate can be used as an amendment; rockwool granulate will add airspace to the existing medium and increase the water-holding capacity. Bag culture is similar to a rockwool slab system, except the plants are placed directly in the bags.

Propagation Cubes

2" x 2" x 2" - 50 cubes per pack

Used to germinate seeds. Highest germination rate of products tested.

Clone Blocks

3" x 3" x 3" - 20 blocks per pack

Suggested for cuttings. Poly-wrapped for extended growth before transplanting.

Growing Slabs

3' x 8" x 3"

Designed to use with 3" x 3" clone block, poly-wrapped for completion of growth cycle.

Bulk Bags

3.85 cubic feet

Loose rockwool for use in bags, pots, and as a replacement medium. Expands to 25 gallons.

HYDROPONIC NUTRIENTS

Selecting the appropriate nutrients for your hydroponic system is an important task. Some species—like lettuce, eggplant, and spinach—require high nitrogen levels to produce lush vegetative growth, but require a lower level of nitrogen to set and ripen their fruit. Bell peppers, herbs, and tomatoes need lower levels of nitrogen during growth after the first five weeks. Match the nutritional needs of your crop by selecting the mix that is best for your crop and system. An excellent book on this subject is *Hydroponic Food Production* by Howard M. Resh (it can be ordered from your local bookstore).

The concentration of nutrients in water is measured on a numerical scale of parts per million (ppm). This number basically tells you how much fertilizer is dissolved in your water. By closely monitoring this concentration you can maintain the best level of nutrients to meet your crop's requirement. To measure this you will need a PPM meter. You also use the PPM meter to gauge when it's time to fill your hydroponic system with a fresh mix. Generally, young plants prefer concentrations around 300 to 500 ppm, while established or fast-growing plants need levels around 1000 to 1300 ppm.

GROWING TOMATOES

There are three main ways to grow tomatoes commercially in your greenhouse: in large pots or bags directly in greenhouse soil, or hydroponically on a cement floor greenhouse. Hydroponic systems can be as simple as a water emitter dripping a balanced fertilizer mixture to the base of plants growing in a slab of rockwool.

A very profitable way to grow tomatoes is to prepare the ground soil of your greenhouse by growing any good cover crop, such as rye, alfalfa, or oats. Plow this in, tilling two ways. Then spread the recommended rate of fertilizer or approximately 300 bushels of cow manure. Grow a second cover crop–if possible, a different one–and plow again. Also, till each row the length of the greenhouse. Start seeds for your spring crop between January 1 and 15. Transplant in 10 weeks, 1' to 2½' apart. Depending on how prepared, rows should be 16" to 36" apart. Keep day temperature between 70° and 75°F and night temperature between 65° and 67°F. Sow fall crops between June 1 and 15. Transplant July 6 to 15; no later than August 5.

To prevent common diseases:

❖ Greenhouse topsoil must be fumigated each season.

❖ If suckers are removed with a knife, sterilize the knife in chlorine between each plant.

❖ Never grow greenhouse tomatoes next to outdoor tomatoes or peppers in the same season.

❖ Keep all trash, including culls, away from greenhouse.

A cup of a phosphorus/calcium mixture is mixed in each planting area. A full greenhouse can easily be planted in one day with two people.

As soon as plants are planted, it's a good idea to use an upstart root stimulator solution. One of my favorite additives for this upstart root stimulator is indole butric acid.

Now construct a drip irrigation system with emitters at each plant (see irrigation supply houses for directions). By using a fertilizer injection system with an appropriate blend you will have the best watering system for tomatoes. Most nursery supply houses carry the hydroponic mix for the type of vegetables you will grow.

Lay a mulch of black plastic between rows, being careful to cut slits or holes for young tomatoes, squash, cucumbers, colored bells, hot and green peppers, basil, lettuce, and so on. Just about all short season crops can be grown successfully year round.

Tie tomatoes at the base and support them to overhead supports, twisting the growing stems around the string as they grow (about once a week). Suckers that are growing tips between the stem and limbs should be picked off weekly also.

Plants should be sprayed weekly with an insect repellant, and twice monthly with Dipel® for tomato worms.

Pollination can be achieved by shaking plants at the first sign of blooms, then daily for about three days. Tomatoes need to be pollinated between 11 a.m. and noon for best results. Flowers do like rather high humidity for pollination, so—if you must—mist the plants twice during the time you shake them. Harvest daily and pick off any deformed or damaged fruit. All colors and degrees of ripeness are in great demand, especially during cold months. Try yellow, plum, speckled, and cherry tomatoes. Once you find a good market you'll stay sold out and enjoy profits of your choice.

HYDROPONICS

Production costs (supplies, fuel, overhead, packing, shipping, labor) will amount to about $3,000 each 3,000 sq. ft. house for crops such as tomato or cucumber. Major supplies required for production include fertilizer, heating fuel, pH and conductivity meters, seeds, starting blocks for seedlings, pesticides, sprayer, trellis string and plant clips, harvesting containers, packing boxes, and wrapping materials. Overhead costs include electricity for lights, pumps, heaters, and fans; insurance, taxes, and similar expenses.

1991 was an excellent year for hydroponic tomato growers. Cold temperatures in Florida in early spring may have been responsible, as the Florida tomatoes were in short supply and the prices were quite high. This allowed hydroponic growers to get a premium over the year before.

Wholesale prices in Ohio averaged $1.21 per pound over the entire year (figuring the low summer prices as well as the higher spring prices). Growers in the New England states did even better, with average prices near the $2 mark.

Lettuce continues to be a steady crop, with fairly consistent prices throughout the year. Hydro bibb growers in the Ohio area are receiving a steady 50¢ a head, which seems to be fairly common throughout the Midwest. East Coast growers get slightly more. Herbs are gaining favor with hydroponic growers, with more growers devoting a section of their greenhouses to them alongside the bibb lettuce.

Greenhouse tomatoes are indeterminate, which means they grow and produce fruits continually. Therefore, the greenhouse tomato plant may reach 20 or more feet in length, requiring trellising. Fruit must be picked frequently (as often as every other day) to maintain the desired maturity and quality.

Peppers and lettuce grown in the greenhouse are different from those grown in the field. These two crops require more exacting environmental conditions for optimum growth and quality than tomatoes and cucumbers. High temperatures (above 85°F) can reduce fruit set of pepper, and can lead to bitter-tasting lettuce.

Crop production and maintenance requires several manhours per greenhouse every day. Management operations include formulating fertilizer solutions, checking greenhouse operations such as heating and cooling, pruning and tying the crop, pollinating tomatoes, spraying for pest control, cluster-pruning tomatoes, harvesting, grading, packing, transporting, and accounting bookwork. All of these operations must be done precisely on time. Therefore, the grower must be committed to doing a good job of management or have competent labor. Attention to detail will separate the good growers from the poor ones.

One advantage of growing tomatoes under greenhouse conditions is the ability to pick small quantities of ripe fruit every day or so (rather than harvesting great quantities during a minimum number of pickings). The growth characteristics of greenhouse fruits demand close and careful handling by harvesters.

In general, growers should be wary when selling their product and should be aware that (advance) contracts are very rare in the produce industry. This is because prices depend upon conditions that change frequently or that are relative rather than absolute. Supply and quality conditions from other sources heavily influence the price a producer is offered. In addition, producers cannot predict the quality of their own harvest, or even its quantity. (This is more feasible, however, with greenhouse production than with field production).

Although not foolproof, growers should check to see whether or not a broker (or any buyer) is bonded in your state. The buyer or handler should also be checked by referring to some type of directory such as the Redbook. Producing a high quality product is not enough; it must be marketed successfully in order to consider the production cycle a success.

In any fertilization system, the basic components are stock tanks for fertilizers, a water source, a method of mixing fertilizer and water in correct proportion, and a pump to move the water and fertilizer mix to the plants. The method in which these components are arranged and used depends on the specific cultural system used.

In all systems, it is important to be sure the fertilizer is formulated properly. The grower must mix the correct amount of fertilizer so that the plants receive the right concentration (ppm) of the various nutrients.

BAG CULTURE

Bag culture is a production system where greenhouse vegetables are grown in a soilless mix contained in a polyethylene bag. The bag can be sealed around the mix or it can be an open-top bag. The closed bags are laid flat on the greenhouse floor, with plants growing from planting holes in the sides of the bags. These are called "lay-flat" bags. The open-top or "upright" bag system involves growing a single plant in a bag filled with mix. In either system, about ½ to ⅔ cu. ft. of media mix should be made available for each plant.

Media for the bags can be peat/vermiculite, sawdust, rockwool, rice hulls, pine bark, peanut hulls, or various mixtures. Bags can be purchased at greenhouse supply houses (most household garbage bags are not strong enough). The bags are filled with the desired sterile mix and placed in double rows in the house. Transplants are produced in a soilless mix, such as peat/vermiculite or rockwool, and transplanted into the bags, usually one plant per bag. The

Young tomato plants in the perlite bag system.

soilless mix usually contains some fertilizer to start the plants.

Bags are irrigated and fertilized through a micro (drip) system in which a polyethylene pipe delivers water and fertilizer down the double row of bags, and each bag is irrigated from an emitter and piece of spaghetti tubing. Many types of emitters are available. Choose one that will wet the entire bag of mix.

Lay-flat bags contain the media, usually peat/vermiculite or rockwool mixes, in a totally closed bag. Growers can make their own bags, but most often these bags are purchased prepared. Bags are made of 4-mil, ultraviolet stabilized polyethylene. The cost of new bags would be approximately $3 to $5 each, depending on the size and quantity purchased.

Bags are laid out in double rows in the greenhouse and drip irrigation lines are installed. Depending on the size of bag and volume of mix, two or three tomato plants can be accommodated in each lay-flat bag. Plants are produced in peat/vermiculite mix or rockwool cubes and transplanted into the bags. An alternative is to grow transplants in "bottomless" or mesh-bottom pots, which are set into the bags. Drainage slits are needed in the bottom edge of the bags so that excess solution can be removed.

The main advantages of bag culture include ease of handling, sterilizing new median is unnecessary, reduced risk of spread of waterborne Pythium root rots in the house, and the capability of a "buffer" for water and fertilizer in case of power outages.

FORMS FOR GROWING

Slabs for tomatoes are commonly 3" thick, 6 to 8" wide, and 36" long. Other sizes are available, depending on the crop. Slabs are packaged in white or white-on-black polyethylene sleeves. Depending on the source and quantity, each slab costs about $2.50 to $3.50.

Rockwool slab culture is similar to bag culture in greenhouse layout and operation. Slabs are laid in twin rows and irrigated by micro-irrigation with one emitter per plant. Transplants are started in small rockwool cubes, and then the cubes are placed in larger transplant blocks (approximately 3" square). The blocks with the transplants are then placed in the greenhouse on the slabs where the plant will eventually root into the slab media. Two or three tomato plants can be grown per 36" slab. It is possible to achieve average populations of 2½ plants per slab by rooting plants over the end-to-end junction of two slabs. Half of the root system is in each slab.

Fertilization of rockwool is accomplished by through the drip irrigation system. Fertilizer is applied with each irrigation event. The controller is preset for a timed irrigation event (e.g., two or three minutes), and it opens a solenoid valve to start the flow of water and fertilizers. In most systems, water is mixed with fertilizer stock solution in a 1:100 ratio before it is applied to the slabs. Simple proportioning pumps can do this task for most greenhouse operations without the need for complicated injectors.

A "start tray" monitors the feeding of the plants and signals the injectors to feed on demand.

Rockwool culture has many advantages over other production systems. Among these are ease of handling, installation, and slab removal. Rockwool has a high water-holding capacity and allows for more precise control of nutrients. Each slab is inert and sterile, and rockwool systems offer predictable performance. Rockwool has very high air pore space, which provides higher oxygen levels and thus better root growth than the nutrient film tubes (which is the old way). However, the most important advantage of the rockwool system is that it is not a recirculating system, such as NFT. Each slab is "containerized," and nutrient solution does not flow from one slab to another and back via a sump tank. This closed type of system reduces the risk of spreading a disease pathogen such as Pythium root rot. Rockwool culture is also considerably less labor intensive than NFT since the rockwool irrigation and fertilization are automatically managed by the starter tray and proportioners.

WATER QUALITY FOR GREENHOUSE VEGETABLES

Greenhouse tomatoes require as much as two quarts water per plant daily. Maximum requirements exist when the plants are full grown and there are high solar radiation and high temperatures. The irrigation system should be capable of delivering adequate amounts of water to all parts of the greenhouse. The pump and irrigation delivery system must be designed so that enough water can be delivered to each plant in the house during peak consumptive periods.

Electrical conductivity (EC), measured as decisiemens per meter ($dS.m^{-1}$) is an estimate of the total soluble salt (solids) content of the water. Water with an EC value greater than 1.5 $dS.m^{-1}$ (same as 1.5 mmhos per centimeter [mmhos.cm^{-1}]) is considered to be poor quality for most greenhouse crops.

The pH of the media refers to the concentration of hydrogen ions (H+) in the media solution. The concentration is determined by a pH electrode, or can be approximated by a pH color-strip paper dipped into the solution. The pH of the media solution is important because certain plant nutrition aspects are influenced by pH, such as solubility of essential elements. Most elements are absorbed best from a media with a pH of 5.5 to 6.5.

Excessive amounts of fertilizer in the media can lead to soluble salt burn, especially on young plants or seedlings. Salt burn is the result of damage to the roots by desiccation. High salt concentrations in the media reduce the roots' capability of taking up water. Reduced water uptake is due to the tendency of water to move away from the root toward the higher osmotic potential (salty) area in the media. Tomatoes generally tolerate higher salt conditions than cucumbers, peppers, or lettuce.

High soluble salt levels are especially dangerous in the early fall and late spring seasons, because high temperatures and high solar radiation lead to increased water demand by the plants. In general, growers in the South should not try to explicitly follow fertilizer programs used in Northern climates. Northern fertilizer programs tend to rely on levels of fertilizer that often prove to be excessive under Southern conditions.

Damage to roots and plant stems caused by soluble salt burn leads to secondary invasion by pathogenic fungi and resulting rot. Evaporation of water can leave behind dried salt deposits that may clog emitters.

Control of soluble salt damage begins with correct formulation of the nutrient solution. The grower should monitor the EC of the nutri-ent solution as it is delivered to the plant. This will serve as an indicator that the nutrient solution was probably formulated correctly. Also, the EC of the growing media should be checked to ensure that EC is not building to damaging levels.

In rockwool, the EC in the slabs should not vary more than 0.3 EC units dS.m^{-1} above or below the EC of the applied nutrient solution.

Once it is determined that the nutrient solution EC is too high, the only recourse is to flush the system and apply a new nutrient solution of correct EC and nutrient content. Flushing should be done with water of a weak nutrient solution.

The EC meter should be carefully calibrated using a high quality conductivity standard. The small hand-held meters in common use require regular calibration to remain accurate. These meters are not error-free or maintenance-free, and inaccurate measurements may result if they are not checked every week or two.

For growers who may not be aware of it, Crop King Inc. offers a custom blend nutrient program. It is very useful for growers who have water that is less than ideal. If this is of interest to you, provide them with your water analysis and some basic information, and they'll provide you with a recipe formula based on your crop, water, and other factors.

Crop King, Inc. also has a vegetable marketing division that will help in finding buyers for your produce.

TRANSPLANT PRODUCTION

Greenhouse tomato crops are started from transplants to ensure uniform crop establishment. One of the keys to successful crops is high quality transplants, and each grower must be careful to do everything possible to ensure that the highest quality plants are set in the production house. Disease transmission is the biggest concern.

Seedlings will emerge in about 7 to 10 days. The seedlings should be moistened with the nutrient solution until they are ready to be transplanted to the production house. About 3 to 4 weeks are needed to produce a minimal size plant (about 4-6" tall) ready for transplanting. Individual seedlings may need to be separated from the cube mat and spaced out in trays to prevent etiolation (spindly plants).

ENVIRONMENTAL CONTROL

Temperature management is very important for successful tomato crops. Poorly controlled temperature regimes can increase disease problems. Tomatoes produce the largest yields of highest quality fruits when day temperatures are in the range of 80°F to 85°F, and when night temperatures remain between 62°F and 72°F.

Excessive temperatures can lead to poor fruit color (orange instead of deep red). High localized fruit temperatures (sun scald or sunburn) from excessive radiant energy on fruits can lead to yellow areas that never turn red. This symptom is referred to as "solar yellows." Unmarketable fruit is the result. On some cultivars that have the "green shoulder" genetic background, excessive fruit temperature seems to enhance the green shoulder expression. Often, these fruits will not develop uniform red color, and the shoulders become rough and cracked. High temperatures (above 90°F) also result in poor pollination and reduced fruit set.

The majority of cooling on warm, dry days is achieved by exhaust fans and evaporative cooling pads. Shading by greenhouse shade paint or cloths is needed to reduce the heat load in fall and spring when temperature and humidity are high. Shade cloths (white or reflective)

installed in the house above the trellis are more flexible than the white greenhouse shading paint.

The degree of shading ranges from about 20% early to about 50% during the hottest part of the season. The plastic greenhouse cover alone can shade anywhere from 10 to 20% depending on type and age.

SEQUENCE OF OPERATIONS FOR TOMATO CULTURE

A. Production area
   1. Set up benches and disinfect with 5 to 10% bleach solution.

B. Seeding
   1. Drop seeds singly into the predrilled holes in the cubes, dampen with plain water adjusted to pH 6.0, place in the germination area, and check regularly for moisture.

   2. Once sprouted, place seedlings under optimum light and temperature.

C. Transplant care
   1. Seedlings will emerge in 8 to 10 days.

   2. Moisten with diluted nutrient solution until ready to be transplanted.

   3. Inspect regularly for insects and disease.

D. Preparing the greenhouse
   1. Greenhouse needs to be cleaned and in operational readiness.

   2. Nutrient solution delivery system needs to be flushed and checked for operational efficiency. Clean filters. Check flow rates, install cable and strings.

   3. Check greenhouse environmental control system, thermostats or controllers, alarm systems, fan motors and belts, furnaces, blowers, heat distributing tubing, and vents.

E. **Transplanting**

1. Transplants 4 to 6" tall are ready to go to the greenhouse. For rockwool or bag culture, seedlings can go from the 4" stage to the production stage without additional time in the seedling area.

2. Dilute nutrient solution for early season.

3. Place in media and begin nutrient solution flow.

4. Place transplant blocks for the rockwool system on the slab through cross-slits, and place the irrigation emitter on top of the block with the flow of water directed at the block, not the plant stem. Set controller to deliver about 150 mls (1.3 pint) solution per slab per irrigation event.

5. Set exhaust fans for 78°F to 85°F. Set cooling pad thermostat at about 80°F.

6. Night temperatures should be maintained at or above 62°F. Pulsing outside air into the greenhouse by a timer on the jet-fan vent will help reduce humidity in the house during the night.

7. Inspect for plugged emitters.

8. Inspect for insects or disease and initiate control programs.

9. Check nutrient solution level. Check the EC level in the peat bag systems and in rockwool system.

10. Keep records of EC, pH, temperature.

11. As soon as flowers appear, begin pollination. Pollinate between 10 am and 3 pm.

12. Remove suckers as soon as they reach 2 to 3" in length.

13. Attach plant clips when plants reach 12 to 15" tall and start to tip. Clip or tape and sucker plants regularly.

14. At first or second cluster, lean the plants slightly by moving twine down the trellis cable a foot or so. This will prepare the plant stem for the leaning and lowering process so that stem breakage is reduced.

F. **Growing the crop**

1. Increase nutrient concentration. The EC of this solution will be in the range of 1.0–1.3. Nitrogen concentration should be about 90-100 ppm.

2. As plants reach the cable, about five clusters will be present and harvest will begin. Harvest tomatoes at least 3 times weekly for most of the season.

3. Remove lower leaves and lower the plants approximately every 2 weeks.

4. Check plants for insects and diseases.

5. Continue pollinating, pruning, suckering, clipping (or taping), etc.

6. After the fifth cluster, increase nutrient solution concentration to higher rate.

G. **Terminating the crop**

1. Cease pollination about 40 to 45 days prior to termination date.

2. Top plants (clip terminal bud off) 40 to 45 days prior to termination date.

3. Continue fertilizing and harvesting.

4. Cease irrigation 3 to 5 days prior to plant removal to help dry out the slabs and make them easier to handle.

5. Clip plants at the base and remove to a burial area. Remove rockwool slabs and sterilize prior to reutilization.

6. Remove all plant material and clean greenhouse and growing surfaces.

7. Flush and clean irrigation systems.

8. Between crops, inspect and perform maintenance duties on the greenhouse and operational systems.

OPTIMAL HARVEST FACTORS

To maximize storage life, crops must be harvested at the appropriate stage of growth or maturity.

The United States Department of Agriculture has published grade standards for greenhouse-grown tomatoes, cucumbers, leaf lettuce, and sweet peppers. The standards cite tolerances, defects, and packing requirements that must be met by the shipper in order for a container to be legally labeled with a governmental grade such as U.S. Fancy, U.S. #1, etc. Grade standards for individual commodities can be obtained from the USDA.

Leaf lettuce is harvested when the leaves are of typical color for the type being grown, not wilted, and free from defects such as tip burn. The entire plant can be harvested and placed directly into individual containers or plastic sleeves. Roots should be rinsed free of any soil, media, etc. By keeping the roots moist, wilting can be minimized during subsequent handling. The roots can also be trimmed at harvest. Pick cucumbers without stems at the appropriate development stage; pick peppers and tomatoes with stems attached.

Cucumbers and peppers require frequent, multiple harvests in order to supply a uniformly mature product with optimal quality to the desired market.

Tomatoes are also harvested in this manner when there is some color showing on the surface, usually the breaker (less than 10% color) or turning (10 to 30% color) stage. Multiple harvests necessitate attentiveness on the part of the greenhouse manager and a reliable supply of labor.

Harvest during the early morning hours to avoid accumulation of additional "field heat." Use proper harvesting techniques to minimize injury. Workers should trim fingernails closely to reduce punctures. Grasp peppers so they detach with the stems intact. At harvest, carefully place crops in single or double layer containers to avoid bruising. Once filled with the harvested crop, quickly but carefully transport containers to the packing shed to reduce mechanical injuries such as bruises, abrasions, and cuts. Injuries provide sites for decay infection later during handling and marketing.

PRECOOLING AND STORAGE

Cucumbers and peppers should be cooled to 50°F (10C). Tomatoes which are at the breaker or turning stage should not be cooled below 55°F (12C), while tomatoes at the pink to light red ripeness stages may be stored successfully at 50°F (10C). Holding these vegetables at temperatures lower than recommended during precooling or during refrigerated storage or transport can cause "chill injury."

PRODUCTION SANITATION FOR DISEASE CONTROL

A number of recommended sanitation steps have been adopted by successful growers. Some of the more common ones are listed below.

1. Add an "air lock" type entrance to each production house so workers, wind-carried insects, and soil do not enter the production area directly from the outside.

2. Use foot baths to prevent non-sterile soil from being carried into the production space.

3. Restrict access to production and transplant houses.

4. Raise transplants to a height of at least 1' above the ground.

5. Prohibit cigars, cigarettes, snuff, and chewing tobacco in production areas.

6. Establish rigid hand-scrubbing rules for

personnel involved in pruning, pollinating, tying, or harvesting activities.

7. Use filters on all intakes to restrict air-blown soil and vector-insect entry.

8. Maintain rigid vegetation control around the perimeter of the houses to avoid insect and pathogen build-up on weeds.

9. Perform periodic tool, walkway, and bench surface treatment with disinfectants.

SPECIALIZE IN PEPPERS

Hot and sweet peppers are rapidly increasing in popularity and becoming the most popular garden plant next to tomatoes. Peppers are extremely healthy for people to eat every day, and are a great seasoning for foods instead of salt or butter.

Sales of peppers have increased approximately 20% each year for the last three years, and show no signs of slowing down. Colored bell peppers along with popular hot varieties are the most profitable. Green sweet peppers can also do well if allowed to color up to red. Best-sellers:

Hot	Sweet
Jalapeno	*Purple, Yellow, Bell*
Chili	*Sweet Pickle*
Atomic Missiles	*Banana*
Cayenne	*Pimento Select*
Hot Banana	*Gypsy Hybrid*

These can be grown in 4-packs in trays (the most popular), in 4" pots, or grown out to producing size in 6" pots. A good rich soil is preferred to the sterile soil mix. A balanced 6-6-6 or 14-14-14 fertilizer is ideal. Watch out for aphids and spray weekly.

Peppers are easily grown by the beginner. Single plants or multiplants can be grown together. Pinch tops or hold back watering for a bushy look. Shading will decrease blooms but

produce darker foliage and a more shapely plant. Use a bloom fertilizer after seedlings are 30 days old.

Prepare your greenhouse the same way as for tomatoes, if growing directly in the ground. Transplant young plants when approximately 5" high. Use a transplant drench and mulch with black plastic.

To encourage healthy growth, pick off the first set of blooms. This will let the plant's energy be directed to root and stem growth.

When using a commercial nutrient at the bud development stage of flowering vegetables such as tomatoes, peppers, or cucumbers, it is a good idea to use a formula with a high middle number like 10-20-10. This increased amount of phosphorus will aid healthy root and bud development.

Sow seeds in hot beds, flats, or separate section trays in greenhouse. Germinate in a sterile medium like Jiffy mix at 70° soil temperature for 14 days. Plant ¼" deep, and transplant into pots when leaves are ⅜" in diameter. Grow at 70°F; reduce soil moisture slightly to harden. Keep night temperature above 62°. Nights colder than this will cause blossoms to drop, producing huge bushy plants without peppers. Removing early fruits and blossoms can also increase total yield by 25%.

Bacterial diseases are often caused by secondary sources, not the seed. Be especially careful of the following sources of disease:

❖ Infections by insects from diseased tomatoes.

❖ Second use of porous foam transplant trays that have not been sterilized.

❖ Secondary infection from weeds or host plants.

❖ Use of cultivation equipment during wet periods.

❖ Previous crop soil infection by diseased plants.

❖ Insects who invade greenhouses and pass diseases indoors.

❖ Use of improperly sterilized soil.

Experiment with different varieties of sweet and hot peppers. Many new types are becoming very popular.

Pepper plants sell well everywhere, especially at local nurseries, department stores, vegetable markes, and groceries. Fresh-picked peppers bring an added profit. Purple, yellow, and red bells bring about 50¢ to $1.00 each wholesale. Jalapeno chiles are usually $2.00/lb. or by the box at the going daily rate.

CUCUMBERS

Greenhouse or forcing cucumbers are finding increasing favor. The European or English cucumbers are gynoecious (all female). The seeds remain very small and are not bitter. Greenhouse cucumbers produce without pollination and should be kept apart from other cucumbers so that pollination does not inadvertently occur.

Seeds are started and grown on rockwool slabs for top production. Rockwool slabs are usually about 3' long by 8" wide. The system is based on the hydroponic techniques used by the most efficient and quality oriented growers in the world. Commercial growers use rockwool because it is an inert substance, containing only the nutrients in the hydroponic solution, thus providing optimum growth control during the entire crop period. In addition, rockwool helps maintain an ideal air-to-water ratio, resulting in unsurpassed root development. This system can be used for all vegetable crops. Cucumbers are sold by the box; burpless by the count. Select #1 size brings top dollar for regular cucumbers. Longer sizes bring more for burpless.

BEST VARIETIES

Tomatoes (Hybrid Greenhouse Types)
65 to 70 days, 1 oz. = 3,000 to 6,000 plants

Dombito (TMV-VF$_2$ C$_5$)
| 5 -7 ounces | spring or fall |

Jumbo (VFN)
| 5 -8 ounces | spring or fall |

Vision (TMV-VF$_2$ C$_5$)
6 ounces & over fall

Vendor (VFT)
5 ounces & over

Pation Hybrid
| 4 ounces | 50 days developed for container sales |

Trend (TMV-VF$_2$ C$_5$, FCRR)
Fusarium crown rot tolerant

Orange Queen
Bright orange beefstake size fruits

Peppers (Hybrid Sweet)
64 to 760 days, 1 oz. = 4,000 seeds

Bell Tower
| 3-4 lobes | short season |

Bell Captain
| 4 lobes - 4" | long season |

Argo
| 4 lobes - 6" | all seasons |

Purple Bell
| 4 lobes - 4½" | all seasons |

Klondike Bell (Golden)
| 4 lobes - 4½" | all seasons |

Cucumbers (European)
Winter crops start about January 5 to Febuary 1

Sandra
| 16" | summer & fall |

Fall crops start August 1; summer crops May 1 - August 1

Corona
| 16" | cooler 66° at night |

Carmen
Mildew-tolerant for summer or fall production

NATIVE & ORNAMENTAL TREES

There is a growing movement towards mass planting of native and ornamental trees on private and public lands. There are a lot of good markets for selling seedlings in large quantities and landscape size in smaller quantities. Many businesses give away tree seedlings around Earth Day; this really attracts homeowners. One 25-store lumber yard chain gave away over one million seedlings last spring.

Since so many sizes of seedlings exist, it is easiest to price them by asking your local Extension Office for local prices and the size that are in demand. You will find the people in this office to be a wealth of information; use them. They will also know about large orders and who's buying what.

Tree seedlings will take a year to reach a profitable size. The idea is to plant 10,000 or so seeds off to the side of whatever else you are growing. They require hardly any care for 6 months; just keep them moist and warm.

Roots® is a good soil additive that's sprayed on, and is beneficial to all tree seedlings. In fact, Roots® is excellent on all plants, especially organic foods and herbs. Gardener's Supply Co. carries it, along with a great starter tray for beginnings called APS (Accelerated Propagation System). This reusable growing tray is covered with a clear plastic dome that sits on an automatic watering tray. It is a complete mini-greenhouse that includes a reservoir and holds two quarts of water to ensure consistent moisture for your seedlings. It's great for sprouting tree seeds because you can ignore them for several days.

"The environmental movement and hence all of humanity is in desperate need of a return to the ABC's of life: awareness, balance, and cooperation," according to Adam Roger, editor of *Earth News,* an outstanding magazine that started as a forest restoration newsletter (5126 Clareton Drive, Suite 200, Angora Hills, CA 91301).

Growing trees for cities to plant around public buildings and roads will be a big business in 1992. Start tree seeds in flats or 2¼" pots. This will be determined by the type you grow. Seeds that sprout fast (2 weeks) can be planted in trays, then transplanted to separate pots. Longer germinating seeds like hickory pine, birch, oak, maple, and walnut can be planted in taller pots. Bottom heat from heating pads will increase and speed germination if cool weather is expected.

Feed weekly with ⅓ strength liquid fertilizer and recommended amount of slow-release. Use Safer® Soap Insecticide every 3 or 4 weeks. Transplant when roots are heavy around the edge of pots to 1-gallon or 3-gallon sizes, depending on how long you want to keep them. Give tree seedlings plenty of room for roots to grow. Never let roots start winding around the inside of the pot.

Trees will be a hot item in 1992, so plant at least 1,000 of them—and preferably 10,000. Before you know it these will be the pride of your nursery. Some good sellers are dogwood, weeping willow, maple, magnolia, sweet gum, sycamore, pine, oak, cedar, walnut, hickory, and fruit trees. When growing seedlings, always keep moist and shaded in a warm area of 70° to 80°F until sprouted. This can be in your basement, attic, yard, or greenhouse. I saw some started in an old mobile home that was easy to heat. Sowing tree seeds is the same as any other seed, but they can be hurried along by soaking them, then refrigerating for one month, then planting.

One soil idea for trees is to have your local tree services with grinders dump as many loads as they can. After rotting for one year, this makes great soil when mixed with sand. You can easily fill thousands of 3-gallon and 5-gallon pots at almost no cost.

SPECIAL OCCASION CROPS

Poinsettias for Thanksgiving and Christmas are the bestseller, followed by Easter lilies and hydrangeas for Easter, then azaleas and violets for Mother's Day. All large growers seem to grow at least one of these in large volume (10,000 or more), and take great care to make sure they are blooming at the right week. Most stores will buy these one month before the delivery date, and the larger chains will buy every day until the day before the holiday.

Growing a large quantity of 8" and 10" hanging baskets for Mother's Day is a sure seller. Foliage baskets as well as blooming flowers are the bestsellers. Herbs, planted three to five different varieties in one hanging basket, are a new idea that goes over very well.

TROPICAL FRUITS

Tropical fruit plants are another top item for beginners. Seeds are easily accessible. Buy the fresh fruits (papaya, kiwi, avocado, lime, guava, etc.), clean and plant, usually in trays, then transplant two-week-old seedlings into separate pots 6" or larger. Osmocote® 14-14-14 is a good fertilizer for all fruits. A large amount of store traffic can be generated at a retail nursery by having regular specials on tropical fruit plants.

Grapes

Varieties for your area can be obtained through your local extension office or specialized nurseries. Grow for produce, winemaking, preserves, juice, or potted rooted cuttings. Grapes have an excellent market with an unlimited demand in most areas. Advertising through local media should bring overwhelming results. Growing conditions are fairly easy to accommodate. Quality flavor can be achieved with differ-

ent amounts and quality of fertilizer. Start at least 100 cuttings of a few different varieties in 6" pots with a sterile potting mix like Pro Mix, Metro Mix, Jiffy, etc. Price at the high side of the local market price, usually about $2.00 to $3.00 for each 6" size pot.

Kiwi

The kiwi is a vigorous climber that has been grown in China for a few thousand years, and is relatively new to the United States.

The plants are very attractive. The stems are covered with red felt-like hairs, and the vines bear 6" to 8"-wide leaves that fall off in the winter. Small yellow flowers show up in April through June, and fruit covered with short brownish fuzz appears in the fall.

Commercial growers use one male to seven females on a sturdy trellis. Try growing directly in the ground of greenhouse or in a large tub for fruit sales.

Kiwis will need pollinating in the greenhouse by collecting pollen from a male plant (male plants grow pollen readily) using a small paintbrush. Gently brush the female flowers twice in one week.

Kiwis grow from seeds that are easily obtained from the ripe fruit. Remove seeds, dry a couple of days, then plant in tray with pH of 7 sterilized seeding mix. Transplanted to 6" pots, vines can grow to 14' in one season and produce hundreds of fruits. Small plants are now in demand at local nurseries and department stores. Contact them first. Fruit sells with no trouble to local or national groceries or farmer's market. Keep moist and well fed.

Bananas

This is my favorite of the tropical fruit plants. The best way to start these is to purchase tissue culture starts from wholesale nurseries for about 40¢ each. These can be grown to a nice

5' plant in about half the time of most tropical plants. Demand is unbelievable, since there are not many major growers growing these marketable, easy-to-grow plants. Decayed leaves are a good organic fertilizer, the highest potassium level of any leaves. Grow a couple of varieties of both dwarf and regular size. They need lots of water; good organic, rich soil; and full sun. Large 10-gallon pots approximately 6' high sell for $10.00 to $25.00 each wholesale.

Edible Figs

The fig is an interior designer's dream, being lush with large, dark green, long-stemmed leaves.

Figs can be grown quickly from cuttings which root very easily. Take 4" cuttings from young shoots and plant in separate 4" pots. In about one month plants will be well rooted and ready to be sold or transplanted to large pots.

When growing to larger potted plant sizes or growing for fruits, it is far better to thin out limbs than to actually prune them. Avoid fertilizers with excessive nitrogen content. The best varieties are Brown Turkey, Mission, Celesta, and Kadota.

ALL-TIME FAVORITES

Aloe

The aloe family has over 300 members, varying in shape and size. Many are natives of Africa, especially Madagascar. Since ancient times, the thick sap of the exotic aloe plant has been used both for its cosmetic and first aid value.

Aloe should be watered so as to keep the leaf rosette as dry as possible. Water here can cause rot. Do not overwater. Like all succulents, a period of drought will strengthen the plant.

The flower stems grow up from the rosette of leaves. Flowers are orange-red or yellow, bell-shaped, and have a faint fragrance.

Propagate by dividing seeds or cuttings. Dividing off small plants from stock plants when they reach nearly 4" high can be profitable. Seeds will take awhile to grow, but will pay off if a large quantity of plants (1,000) is wanted.

Bird of Paradise

The bird of paradise has become a popular and exotic addition to the home. Because of its colorful appearance and long-lived blooms, these will be a fast seller. Grow the banana-like leafed plant above 55°F. They grow fastest at about 75° to 80°F.

Plant seeds (1 to 6 months to germinate) at 80°. Transplant seedlings at about one month old to a well draining potting soil with 25% additional perlite or vermiculite. Move plants to larger pots as they grow. They will take 2 to 4 years to bloom.

The striking yellow-orange and blue flowers emerge from a green beak-like spike.

Plants require full sun and 14-14-14 slow-release fertilizer for healthy growth.

Let plant dry slightly between watering in spring and summer; reduce water to sparingly in the winter.

Division of smaller size plants at the base during the spring can speed up blooming time to one year for offspring. Tissue culture plugs (1½" size) can be purchased from wholesale nurseries and potted in 6" to 10" pots for a good investment.

The bird of paradise is seldom attacked by insects or disease. Overwatering is usually of greater concern. If stems become brown at the base, stop watering until soil dries out, and use a fungicide if brown area grows larger.

Begonias

Christmas begonias are hybrids between a semi-tuberous type and bulbous type. They have the best features of both parents. They are the most popular variety out of the some 1,000 species and over 10,000 hybrids.

The wax begonia stays in bloom all through the summer. For this reason they are one of the most popular bedding plants, with low, compact, bushy growth. They produce hundreds of flowers during the season.

Colors vary from white, red, to pink; in single and double flowering varieties.

New varieties of F-1 hybrids (Bicola, Electra, Scarlanda) are much healthier and resistant to disease.

Begonias can be grown in full sun or up to 73% shade with good results. Pinch out tips of young plants to promote bushiness, and remove faded flowers and dead leaves to prevent mildew fungus.

Cuttings from stems or leaves are easily made to root with a little root-hormone powder. Use well draining soil, and water only when soil is slightly dry.

During the holidays and through the summer, the bestsellers are usually 6" or 4" pots.

Black-Eyed Susan Vine

Thunbergia alata are easily grown. The bestsellers are in hanging baskets or pots with a trellis. Blooming in June and throughout the summer, the orange flower with a black eye at the center is a fast, easy seller.

Usual growth is basically year round, with no fertilizer needed during the winter.

Thunbergia are fast-growing and need consistent feeding; therefore, water regularly.

Starting smaller plants in slightly cooler weather, such as 60°, is recommended. For June sales, sow seed in March or April.

Cactus

In addition to being popular with cactus collectors, these plants are a favorite with many gardeners. They are fairly easy to grow, needing full hot sun and not much water.

Starting from seed, they will take about three months to germinate. Spread the seeds evenly over a blend of half sand and half regular potting soil. Start seeds in May and keep soil moist but not wet. Once well rooted, allow soil to become dry, then drench thoroughly.

Cactus mildew is the worst problem, causing the base to turn brown and slimy. This can be prevented by not overwatering.

Chrysanthemum

The potted chrysanthemum can be grown and sold year round with good results.

There are many different types of chrysanthemums, which have been bred from numerous hybrids and varieties over the years.

All potted mums should have a healthy, compact appearance, with fresh green leaves and well-developed buds and flowers. "Short day" treatment will be needed to get blooming when needed. Do a lot of research on this one.

Propagating is easiest from cuttings. Purchased from wholesale growers, then stuck down in loose soil in 6" pots, cuttings are misted every 10 minutes to get healthy root formation.

Spider mites and leaf minor may indicate their presence with webs (mites) or a network of scars (leaf minor). Chrysanthemums require some shade, lots of water, and regular feeding.

Diffenbachia

Many varieties of this popular foliage plant exist, all of which are easy to grow and propagate. Diffenbachia come from the rainforests of Columbia and Brazil, and should have growing conditions as close as possible to that. Temperatures around 75°F and high humidity are ideal. They don't like temperatures below 60°F, but can withstand cooler weather without damage.

They need plenty of water in summer, less in winter. Use slow-release fertilizer for this fast, robust grower.

Propagate with cuttings of topshoots, stem shoots, or tissue culture starts.

Bacteria is the only real source of danger and can be avoided by proper watering and occasional fungicide. Spider mites can lead to leaf drop and should be watched for.

Ficus Benjamina/Weeping Fig

This member of the fig family is probably the easiest of all foliage plants to grow and one of the most decorative. They thrive best at 70° to 85°F, and not below 60°F. Grow under 55% to 73% shade to get healthy growth and to acclimate for indoor growing after purchased.

Don't let these dry out. All ficus need plenty of water and a drip system is preferred.

The easiest way to propagate is by top or sideshoot cuttings. Make cuttings 5" or more using a hormone rooting compound, and mist frequently so they don't dry out (approximately every 10 minutes, depending on temperature).

Ficus Elastica/Rubber Tree

The rubber tree is well known as a foolproof beginner's plant. It is very easy to grow and seems to thrive on neglect.

The large, 5" to 12"-long leaves are dark, shiny green, and come in shades to a reddish-brown.

Use tipshoots and stem cuttings with a rooting powder and bottom heat in cooler climates.

Grow at temperatures between 70° and 80°F, with lows above 55°. They need lots of water and fertilizer.

Geraniums

A popular indoor and outdoor bloomer, the geranium is a fast, easy plant to grow.

Propagated mostly by cuttings, seeds, and tissue culture, they are becoming popular with some commercial greenhouses.

Scented geraniums are a great seller, coming in fragrances of lemon, lime, pineapple, rose, cinnamon, coconut, and others. These flowers are rather small, and the foliage is a little nicer than common geraniums.

Put three or more 4" cuttings in each 6" pot in light, porous potting soil. In the spring and summer give lots of water and four hours of sunlight or 73% shade. Use rooting powder in sandy soil for faster rooting.

Blooming can be encouraged by putting plants in cool area (50° to 55°F) for a month, or by reducing light to 9 hours a day for 30 days.

Kalanchoe

Kalanchoes can bloom for months on end without much care at all. They have become very popular and can be found in red, pink, yellow, and orange.

They need little water and fertilizer, and do not like temperatures below 60°F.

Kalanchoe will initiate flower buds only if they are in darkness at least 16 hours a day at temperatures in the 70's in the day and around 60°F at night for at least 30 days.

Chemical growth retardant may be used for bushy growth.

Pothos/Marble Queen

Pothos is a climbing plant with yellow or white variegated pear-shaped green leaves. The ivy-like plant can grow up to 20 feet. Although it can tolerate high temperatures (over 85°F), the leaves are sensitive to moisture, which can lead to discoloration.

Never overwater pothos or marble queen. Let them dry out slightly from time to time.

Temperatures should be 65° to 75°F for best growth, and no lower than 55°F.

Propagate by taking cuttings 4" long with one single leaf attached. Put up to ten of them together in a hanging basket or pot. Misting speeds rooting, but is not needed if the temperature is fairly warm.

Brown spots and leaf edging are signs that the soil is too wet or cold. Spider mites will occasionally attack this plant.

Schefflera

This is my favorite foliage plant. There is always a good market for them, and they are very popular because of their luxuriant green leaves. The leaves are dark green, and are divided into 6 to 14 oval leaflets on a 4" to 6"-long stem. Two main varieties are popular with commercial greenhouses: schefflera actinophylla and schefflera arboricola, which is the dwarf, bushier type.

Propagate from fresh seeds or cuttings. Young plants prefer slightly higher temperatures than adult plants. Ideal is between 60° to 70°F, with 50°F at night.

Scheffleras need lots of water, prefer high humidity, and should have good soil drainage.

Use well draining potting soil mixed with half coarse sand for rooting cuttings.

Scale and spider mites frequently attack these, but have never been a real problem in my greenhouses.

PLANT TISSUE ANALYSIS

Modern growers demand top yields and quality yields. You demand profitable yields. In satisfying these demands, plant tissue analysis has become a valuable crop production tool.

Top quality and profitable yields don't just happen. Many factors must be considered: adequate moisture and fertility, proper plant population, adapted variety, disease and insect resistance and control . . . the list goes on.

One of the most important factors affecting crop yields is the nutrient status of the plant, or the flow of nutrients to plant tissues during the growing season. Nutrient status is an "unseen" factor in plant growth, except when deficiencies become so acute that visual deficiency symptoms appear on the plant.

Plant populations can be counted, and variety names or numbers can be read on the label. Rainfall can be measured with gauges. However, the determination of the nutrient status of plants requires analysis of a plant tissue sample during the growing season.

How can tissue analysis help? A plant tissue analysis will show the nutrient status of the plants during the growing season and it will detect unseen hidden hunger. It can also supply information to confirm visual deficiency symptoms.

Though usually used as a diagnostic tool for future correction of nutrient problems, a plant tissue analysis from young plants will allow for a corrective fertilizer application that same season.

Combined with data from soil analysis, a tissue analysis is an important tool in determining proper fertilizer applications to balance the nutrient availability in the soil and the nutrient requirement of the crop.

A complete tissue analysis will identify the nutrient status of the following elements:

Nitrogen

Aluminum

Sulfur

Manganese

Sodium

Potassium

Copper

Magnesium

Zinc

Calcium

Phosphorus

Boron

Iron

PREPARING YOUR SAMPLE

When gathering the tissue, be sure to use a clean container, one that is not metal (which can contaminate the sample). A paper bag works very well. Collect one pint of clean leaves, air dry, then place in clean paper bags on envelope. Never use a plastic bag for fresh samples! Do not include roots.

RESEARCH

Read more books about greenhouse growing for a preliminary acquaintance with them. Start with the more general texts and progress to specialized subjects, including marketing and business management.

STEP-BY-STEP PLAN OF PRODUCTION

1. PLANTING
   - ❖ Buy pots, fill with good soil and fertilizer
   - ❖ Plant seeds, plugs, or cuttings
   - ❖ Place in appropriate growing area

2. CARE AND GROWING
   - ❖ Water pots every morning (except on rainy days)
   - ❖ Liquid fertilizer feed daily or weekly
   - ❖ Inspect and spray insecticide regularly or when needed
   - ❖ Maximum temperature 90°, minimum temperature 55° for fast growth

3. SHIPMENT PREPARATIONS
   a. Acclimatize if needed
   - ❖ Clean pots and sleeve plants to be boxed
   - ❖ Grade and tag
   - ❖ Pack with growing instructions for retailer

4. PICK-UP OR DELIVERY AND COLLECTING
   - ❖ Pick-up or shipment date
   - ❖ Write out invoice and bill of lading for delivery
   - ❖ Get cash or check on first order, bill after that
   - ❖ Give 2% discount if paid in 10 days, surcharge if over 30
   - ❖ Check all paperwork on both ends and get approximate date for next shipment

PLANNING

The power of organization! The ability to plan your future can be your greatest asset. Operating without a plan is like operating without the main tool you need to accomplish your goals. The more planning that goes into a project, the better your chances of total success. Start with a long-term goal for about two years, a short-term plan for about two to four months, and a plan to reach your two-year goal. A five- to ten-year plan can do a lot to inspire you when times seem a little rough. Your daily accomplishments will soon mount up until you find that you have accomplished a major goal. Then you will have the satisfaction of sitting back and viewing a full greenhouse, knowing the $2,000 you have invested is growing by approximately $200 per day, to $25,000 in three months.

Before starting a plant nursery, plan all the major details you can think of on paper. Consult the nurseries in your area. Take notes on the things they tell you about their operation. Most nursery owners are happy to tell you all about their business. The time you spend looking at others doing their work will pay off greatly. Always try to improve on operating methods. The success you have with your plant business will depend greatly on the time you take to plan and observe your work and others.

GETTING STARTED

The best plants to start with because they are easy and fast-growing are:

HERBS - Basil, sage, parsley, mint, oregano, thyme, chives, catnip, coriander. Start from seeds.

PEPPERS - Missile ornamental, hot, and sweet. Seeds in trays, then transplant to 6" pots.

FALSE JERUSALEM CHERRY - Sell in 1-gallon pots. Seeds grown in trays, then transplant to 6" to 1-gallon pots.

FLOWERS - Marigolds, petunias, impatiens. 4" to 5" pots. Grow from seeds.

POTHOS - Hanging baskets. Take cuttings from stock; 8" to 10" pots.

SELLOUMS - Seeds start in beds or trays; 6" to 10" pots.

SCHEFFLERAS - Seeds start in trays or beds; 1-gallon to 3-gallon pots; 6" to 10" pots.

PORTULACA - Afternoon bloomer. Start seeds in 4" pots; 10" hanging baskets.

SPIDER PLANTS - Grow stock from pups or start with one or more starts. Grow and keep for stock.

COLEUS - Bright colors, 6" pots. Plant seed to get stock plants, then take cuttings.

VEGETABLES - Tomatoes, peppers (purple, chile, jalapeno, bell). Start seeds in trays or bed, transplant to 6" pots.

Section 3
Greenhouses

The reason for building a greenhouse is to get faster growth by raising humidity and controlling temperatures. The idea is to have the right light intensity, high humidity, and optimum temperature for the crop you grow. (This is one reason I believe a beginner can grow large quantities of one or two types of plants faster and more successfully than trying to accommodate the needs of ten different types of plants.)

I suggest that the first year you start some plants in late winter for spring and summer sales, some in spring for summer and fall sales, and test just a few types the first hard winter (below 0°). Get acquainted with your greenhouse and the amount of heat you need without worrying about losing money.

The location of your greenhouse is important and can make a big difference in whether a crop of plants is as profitable as it can be. Plenty of sun and water are the most important priorities when growing most plants. Light can be regulated by shade cloth on a cloudy day when you want as much growth as possible.

It is often said that labor, energy, and capital are the three major cost factors in a typical modern greenhouse production system. For instance, a well-designed double poly greenhouse uses 50% less heating energy than a single layer glass-on-fiberglass house for most crops in most areas. New greenhouses with low-cost inflated double-polyethylene sheet plastics require a much lower investment than the more expensive glass, acrylic, and polycarbonate structured panel greenhouses. However, the more expensive coverings normally have substantially lower annual maintenance and replacement costs.

MAXIMUM LIGHT TRANSMISSION

Maximum light transmission is most important during the darkest days of winter. The rest of the time it may actually be a detriment to production if ventilation is not properly maintained and cared for.

Single glass sheets tend to have the highest light transmission at 90 to 93%. Once the glass is properly framed, the best designed glasshouse will transmit no more than 70% of the light. With wires, heating pipes, and obstacles, light will normally measure no more than 60 to 70% at the crop level. This level can also be achieved with double polyethylene sheets or structured panels of acrylic and polycarbonate, if well-designed framing is used.

ENVIRONMENTAL CONTROL

The importance of a controlled environment in your greenhouse cannot be overestimated. Fresh, moving air is as important to your plants as light and water. Whether you are growing plants in containers or hydroponically, you must pay attention to the temperature and humidity levels. Plants like temperatures at 70° to 75°, and humidity at about 50%. Maintain those levels consistently and your plants will grow faster, with better color and quality.

When climate factors are properly managed (a good climate control computer helps when you are large enough), production in the double poly greenhouses will usually surpass that of a single-glazed or fiberglass greenhouse.

CO₂ ENRICHMENT

Carbon dioxide is necessary for healthy, top quality plants. During the fall and winter, when greenhouses stay closed with no air circulation from the outside, you may want to "turbo charge" plant growth by raising the levels of available CO_2 above normal. Atmosphere concentrations are normally between 250 and 350 ppm. Bringing the level up to 1200 to 1500 ppm can be an amazing stimulant to plant growth, increasing it as much as 30% in most plants.

It is important that your plants be growing at or near peak health for CO_2 enrichment to show its effects. CO_2 enrichment does not replace good growing skills!

TYPICAL GREENHOUSE EQUIPMENT

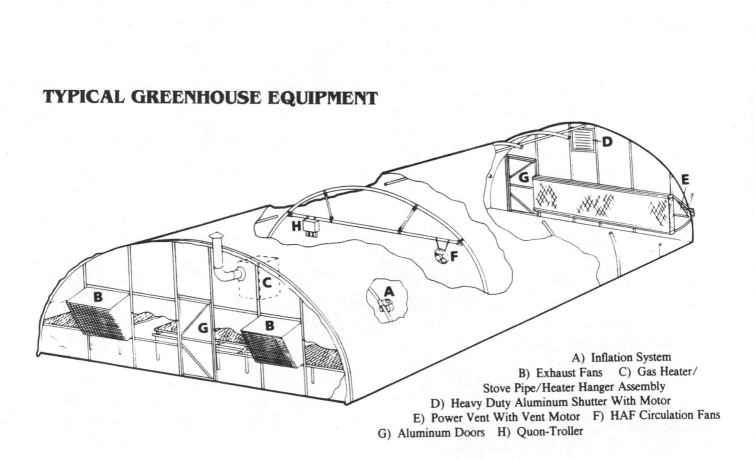

A) Inflation System
B) Exhaust Fans   C) Gas Heater/
Stove Pipe/Heater Hanger Assembly
D) Heavy Duty Aluminum Shutter With Motor
E) Power Vent With Vent Motor   F) HAF Circulation Fans
G) Aluminum Doors   H) Quon-Troller

CHOOSING THE RIGHT GREENHOUSE COVERING

One objective in building a new greenhouse or retrofitting an existing one is to find the best quality covering for your money. In a new or used greenhouse the investment can be substantial, so it pays to consider longevity and permanence. Weigh considerations such as business continuance, maintenance, land value, and energy cost before choosing your covering.

A convenient location on level ground is essential. If you add fill dirt, make a slight crown in the middle to aid drainage. Keep 12' from other greenhouses and other structures. This will allow plenty of air circulation, which is very important.

I studied lots of greenhouses and incorporated several ideas from each which suited my needs best. It is the most efficient one I could build and enables me to produce high quality plants for a low price. (See plans on pages 46-48.)

OTHER IDEAS

If needed, dig a small ditch about 6" deep down the sides to aid water drainage. Large puddles can cause excessive humidity. This may lead to the growth of fungus and bacteria.

Your greenhouse should be built so that it can be closed up tight to keep warm air in and small animals out. When building a greenhouse out of wood, use only pressure-treated lumber and exterior plywood. Galvanized nails are a must. If using a double poly roof, make sure that all corners are fairly smooth. This can be done using a hand plane or sandpaper, or by taking duct tape and putting it over the sharp part of the boards. This will prevent punctures and help your roof last much longer.

WOOD STRUCTURE GREENHOUSE

Pressure-treated wood is probably the most common and least expensive material to use when building a greenhouse. The treated wood must be of high quality and be resistant to both rot and termites. If well constructed, your greenhouse should last 15 years and longer.

Two people can build a 30'x 96' greenhouse, using the 4"x 4" pole constructing method, in four or five days. This consists of poles down the middle and each side 6' apart; then there are 2"x 4"s at the side and 1"x 6"s at the top. Rafters are simply two 2"x 4"x 16's with one 2"x 4"x 14' nailed together to make a 30' span (see plans on pages 46-48).

This structure is covered with two layers of poly (especially made for greenhouses) fastened at the edges and blown up with a small fan that lifts the top layer up to a maximum height of about 1½ to 2' at the center. The insulating factor can save 50% on heating costs and give you an inexpensive but very durable roof (about $300 for a 30'x 96' house). I have seen this type of roof hold up well under strong winds, while a steel hoop greenhouse with fiberglass can be bent in by high winds. Also, it's a lot easier to find and work with the materials for a wood greenhouse.

STEEL STRUCTURE GREENHOUSE

Metal buildings are generally what contractors build if you contact one of the large greenhouse companies. They usually range in price from $2,000 to $20,000, depending on the quality and material used. Again, try to incorporate double poly layers on this type of house. I also suggest not trying to build a steel structure yourself. The frame must be very tight and level to assure lasting quality. Steel greenhouses will

CRITERION
FREE-STANDING GREENHOUSE
Galvanized Steel

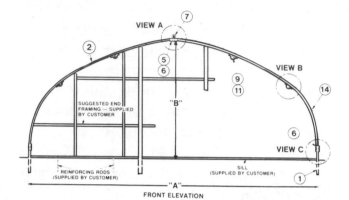

FEATURES:

- Aluminum or galvanized steel frame.
- All parts prefabricated to facilitate installation.
- Heavy duty 1-5/8" O.D. pipe-1-3/8" O.D. rafter bows, posts, purlins and pipe ridges.
- Patented fastening device for connecting the film to the frame.
- All U.S. made parts.

1. 1-5/8" O.D. Ground Post
2. 1-5/8" O.D. Redwood End Bow
3. 1-5/8" O.D. Aluminum End Bow
4. 1-5/8" O.D. Internal Bow
5. Rafter Bow Support
6. Pipe Splice
7. 1-3/8" O.D. Ridge Pipe
8. Ridge Coupling
9. 1-3/8" O.D. Purlin
10. Purlin Coupling
11. Purlin Clasp
12. Male Poly Clamp Extrusion
13. Female Poly Clamp Extrusion
14. Vent Rail (Optional)

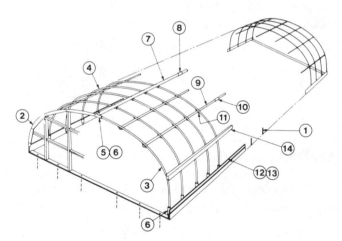

Available Sizes:

Standard widths: 14', 17', 20', 22', 25', 28', 30', in increments of 4' lengths.

14 ft. and 17 ft. houses are constructed of 1" schedule 40 1-piece bows in a semicircular design.

(purlins not included with 14' house)

More Room on Side Walls Than Semi-Circular Greenhouses

Houses with Two Piece Bow Construction

HEIGHT AT INTERVALS	WIDTH = "A" DIM.			
	22'	25'	28'	30'
1 Ft. from Side	5'0'	5'6'	5'6'	5'6''
2 Ft. from Side	6'0'	6'8'	6'10'	6'10''
3 Ft. from Side	6'8'	7'6'	7'8'	7'8''
To Ridge = "B"	9'2'	10'10'	11'4'	11'4''

generally last a very long time—about 30 years. Except for this factor, the cheaper wood frame is just as good. Metal and fiberglass are the best to use if building onto your home. If built with quality craftsmanship, this kind of structure is a desirable addition to any home.

GREENHOUSE COOLING

Most growers use cooling pads to cool greenhouses and speed up plant growth. This may include a large cooling type fan that pulls air through cardboard pads on which water continuously drips, creating an air conditioning effect. The cool air keeps the humidity down, prevents fungus growth, and keeps a constant air evaporation rate. This is important for soil dryness, which must be at just the right level to prevent acid build-up.

The use of cooling fans and pads will reduce the temperature in a greenhouse around 10° to 20° each. But the main reason is for faster plant growth and to reduce chances of fungus growth. The cooling pad/fan system will require hardly any shading and will keep bugs out in spring and summer.

To ventilate in the winter use a perforated poly tube connected to the fresh air inlet. Fans blowing air out will create a vacuum, pulling air into the greenhouse through the tube. The air will be distributed evenly throughout your greenhouse as it blows out the holes in the tube.

One product I have found very useful is Varishade. It is a white paint that gives shade when it's dry. When it gets wet in the rain, it becomes clear, allowing more light in. The average dilution ratio is 4:1 (4 parts water to 1 part paint)—this can be adjusted to create a lighter shading effect. Suppliers of cooling pads, tubes, poly film, blowers, Varishade, and shade cloth are listed in Section 11.

SLOPE (WALL) HOUSING

The slope wall housing allows the shutter to be placed on the intake side of the fan, and eliminates air turbulence that occurs with the shutter on the downwind side of the fan. It prevents the warm air from being lost through the metal wall housing to the outside cold air in cold climate operations.

Acme Kool-Cel™ Evaporative Cooling Pad System

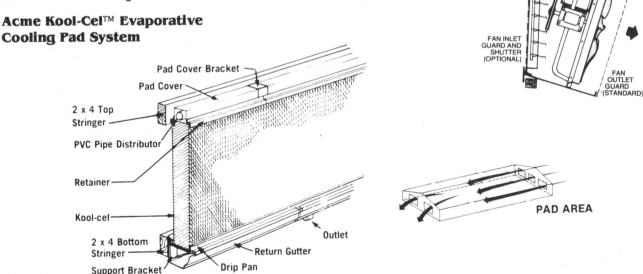

SHADE CLOTH

A large shade house built with 4x4's and 2x4's is all you may need in the beginning. Shade cloth costs about 10¢ per square foot and lasts about ten years.

Shade cloth comes in degrees ranging from 10% to 100% blockout. The most common are 55%, 65% and 73%. I suggest 65% or 73% for top quality foliage plants. Greenhouse cooling is a breeze with 73% of the sun blocked out. You can use 73% in hot summer months and switch to 55% in cooler winter months.

Some greenhouses have curtains that are lowered on the sides to allow complete air circulation. Fans and pads are not used. Curtains running the length and height of the greenhouse are constructed using a reinforced poly material with a 3" hem at the top for galvanized pipe which serves as a rod. Pulleys are installed at every wall support. These are 6' apart on the 4"x 4"s in the type of greenhouse that I recommend. Aircraft cable is used to connect the curtain through the pulley to a main cable, then to a hand crank (boat wench) at the end of that side. To lower or raise one side just turn the crank.

Most of the time in the fall and winter, your greenhouse should be kept closed with just a little bit of air circulation. Maximum air temperature should not exceed 95° for any long period of time. If it does, lay shade cloth on top of the greenhouse to reduce solar heat and cool the interior. If you have the curtain type of greenhouse you can lower the curtains on both sides completely on very hot days and still have efficient air circulation with reduced air temperatures. With this type of greenhouse you may also use a cooling pad system to reduce heat and add moisture on really dry days.

The best arrangement includes both systems: curtains and cooling pads with exhaust fans.

The minimum temperature of foliage plants before growth stops is a bit higher than for other ornamentals. The best growing temperatures range from 60° to 75° at night and 80° to 90° during the day. Maintaining these temperatures in the winter requires accurate heating devices. Air circulation is a major concern under tables and around pots. Putting plants too close can cause improper drying of plants.

Your plants should dry out every day for maximum growth. If you have too much humidity in your greenhouse, you will see drops

SHADE CLOTH

Suggested degrees of shade for plants listed	Snapdragons Chrysanthe-mums Geraniums	Lilies Bedding-Plants Caladiums	Azaleas Begonias Camellias Gloxinias Afr. Violets Poinsettias	Pachysandra Ivy Orchids	Diffenbachia Stag Horn Fern Rhodo-dendron	Fern Anthur-ium Draceanna Philo-dendron
Act. % of Shade	30%	47%	51%	57%	63%	73%

forming on the inside of the walls. This can be overcome by increasing air circulation. You may need to permanently install a strong fan in the wall to circulate fresh air throughout the greenhouse.

GREENHOUSE HEATING

Heating your greenhouse during colder months also helps air circulation. The best method, which also aids circulation, is air or space heating. The combustion units are usually installed inside the greenhouse where they act directly as heat radiators. This type of heating usually requires light oil such as kerosene or propane gas.

FREEZE DAMAGE

Minimize freeze damage to plants outside the greenhouse by spraying them with a liquid polyethylene such as Wilt-Pruf®, Vapor Guard®, or Foliar Gard® the night before cold temperatures are expected. This will slow down thawing and reduce damage.

SOLAR HEATING

One of the simplest ways to create a solar heater that collects, stores, and releases the energy of the sun in your greenhouse is to use 55-gallon drums full of water or stones to support some benches in your greenhouse. Then paint the south side of the drum black and the north side white. As the sun shines all day on the black side, it acts as a collector. When the sun sets at night, the drum releases heat into the air.

HEATING SYSTEMS

Your greenhouse can easily utilize whatever heating system uses the cheapest fuel available. Wood-burning heaters are popular with beginners and should be vented properly. Portable space heaters are often used in warmer climates. Overhead L.P. gas heaters are the most common for all climates. When used with a perforated plastic tube 18" in diameter, that runs the length of your greenhouse, they can be the best method to evenly distribute heat. These heaters are found at most nursery supply businesses.

If using ventilation fans, turn them off a couple of hours before sunset to increase inside heat. This lets you delay using heaters as long as possible.

Other ways to save on fuel are building greenhouses together and using direct heat under tables. Supply houses that sell heaters can help you decide which system is best for your area.

MODINE HIGH EFFICIENCY BLOWER UNIT HEATER

HEATING SYSTEMS

Unit Space Heaters

Unit space heaters are normally fueled with natural gas or fuel oil and use fans for heat distribution. They are often suspended from the greenhouse superstructure, but are sometimes floor mounted. This type of system is fairly easy to install and requires a relatively modest capital investment. Although space heaters that burn propane or natural gas produce CO_2 which can be beneficial to plants, they can also produce combustion byproducts (such as carbon monoxide and ethylene) that can be harmful to both people and plants. To avoid this potential problem, unit space heaters should be vented. Finally, a fresh air intake for each space heater sized to accommodate the unit's burner (usually 6 to 8") is a necessity in tight greenhouses.

Hot Water Systems

Hot water systems utilize piping to provide perimeter or row heating that relies on natural convection to distribute warmed air. Hot water can also be used in overhead fan forced heating systems. Hot water systems require a boiler, valves, and a pressure/temperature-regulated control system. Steam systems are more complex to install and require more maintenance than hot water systems. Although the pipes in hot water systems are slower to heat and cool than steam systems, temperatures are usually more uniform.

Poly-Tube Systems

Poly-tube systems are frequently used in combination with any of the heating units already mentioned to provide more uniform heat distribution, air movement, and ventilation. When poly-tubes are used in a heating system, they are equipped with a heat kit which is a baffled inlet to the fan that inflates the poly-tube. Usually, there are two horizontal discharge heating units located a fixed distance away on either side of the baffle. When the controls (thermostat) call for heating, the unit heaters turn on and blow heated air into the open sides of the baffle. Once the air temperature is raised to the set point level, the heaters stop, but the poly-tube fan continues to circulate air. These systems are also useful for dehumidifying and ventilating with outside air.

In most large (single or gutter-connected) houses, it is best to provide heat via a polyethylene convection tube running the length of the houses. The tube is inflated by a jet fan which receives heated air from the heat source and blows the heated air into the house through the convection tubing.

Placement of the heat distribution tubing should be carefully considered. Traditionally, the tubing consists of one large (30") tube running the length of the greenhouse from the jet fan to the opposite end of the house. This tube is generally about 8' above the ground. As a result, heat is discharged above the plant canopy and much heat is used raising air temperatures high in the greenhouse. A better approach is to discharge the heated air into small 8 to 10" poly tubes placed on or near the floor under the plants. Heat then rises into the plant canopy. Adding a thermal curtain above the trellis in the system can help reduce energy costs.

Heating can be from liquid propane, natural gas, steam, etc. In a single stand-alone house, it is good to use two small heaters, one on each side of the jet fan, instead of one large heater. In this system, freezing of the plants is less likely in case a heater fails. In the double heater system one heater is controlled so it will turn on when the temperature in the plant canopy drops to 65°F. The other heater is set at 62 or 63°F. If the heaters are sized correctly, the greenhouse temperature should not fall below 62°F.

Ventilation

As a practical matter, the only economical methods for cooling greenhouses involve ventilation, which means exchanging greenhouse air for outside air. Ventilation can either be naturally driven by wind and/or temperature gradients (hot air rises) or mechanically created by fans. Although there are several reasons for warm weather ventilation, the most obvious is the control of high temperatures. A properly sized ventilation system can prevent the air temperature inside the greenhouse from rising too high above the outside air temperature.

The reason for high temperatures is the influx of solar radiation through the greenhouse glazing material. The ventilation system must effectively move air directly through the crop and over the floor to prevent excessive temperature build-up around the plants. A generally accepted rule of thumb for greenhouses is that, at a minimum, the ventilation system must be able to provide one air exchange per minute.

EVAPORATIVE COOLING

With ventilation alone, greenhouse temperatures can only be lowered to near outside levels, but with the addition of an evaporative cooling system, greenhouse air can be kept below ambient temperatures. Evaporative cooling works on the principle that at a given temperature the air can hold a certain amount of water vapor. Relative humidity is the percentage of the total water vapor that the air can hold that is actually in the air. When the air is holding all the water vapor that it can, it is saturated and its relative humidity is 100%. If air with relative humidity less than 100% comes into contact with water, some of the water will evaporate into the air. The phase change from water to vapor (evaporation) requires energy (the latent heat of vaporization). This energy is provided by the air, causing its temperature to go down. An evaporative cooling system is comprised of fans for moving the air through the greenhouse and some means of facilitating the evaporation of water into the airstream. Two systems are commercially used: wetted pad and high pressure fog systems.

Wetting Pads

Wetting pad systems are composed of porous material from 2 to 6" thick installed along the greenhouse wall opposite the exhaust fans. Air entering the greenhouse is pulled horizontally through the porous pad material. An upper gutter distributes water evenly to the tops of the pads. Ideally, as the water moves down through the porous pads it spreads over all of the pads' surfaces. As outside air is pulled through the porous material, it comes into close contact with the pads' considerable wetted surface area, which greatly facilitates evaporation. If "perfect contact" between the air and the wetted surfaces were possible, the system would be 100% efficient and the air leaving the pad would be saturated. In practice the most efficient systems provide about 85% of potential cooling. The exact amount of cooling depends primarily on the temperature and relative humidity of the outside air.

There are many types of pads, ranging from low-cost random aspen chip pads to expensive, high-efficiency (85%) cellulose pads.

❖ When possible, locate the pads on the prevailing summer wind side and the fans on the downwind sides of the greenhouse.

❖ The exhaust fans should not discharge toward the pads of another house unless they are at least 50' apart.

❖ The maximum distance from pad to fan should not exceed 200'; distances under 150' are most effective.

- Arrange the pads in a continuous section along the entire wall opposite the exhaust fans. A gap such as a doorway can cause a "hot spot" up to 8 times the width of the gap.

- Provide shutters for closing the pad section during times when heating is required instead of cooling.

- Construct a tight house and keep it tight. Do not leave doors or vents open when the pad system is operating because air moves along the easiest flow path.

- Provide screens on the pads to keep out insects.

Fog Systems

Fog systems operate under high pressure to generate a large percentage of tiny water droplets that remain suspended in the air rather than falling as mist droplets do. To obtain fog requires specially designed nozzles, and pressures between 500 and 1000 psi.

Ideally, the fog droplets remain suspended in the air until they evaporate. For this reason a fog system has the potential of providing a very efficient means of evaporatively cooling a greenhouse. Lines of nozzles can be distributed across the length of the greenhouse and operated in stages to achieve very even humidity distribution. As with the evaporative pads, high pressure fog systems must be operated in conjunction with ventilation fans.

High-pressure fog systems are much more sophisticated than evaporative pad systems and require considerably more maintenance. Reliability of components can vary, often as a function of price. The factor that accounts for most failures is water quality. Purity of water varies considerably among locations, and each water

source should be tested and handled according to recommended test results. With very few exceptions, water must be treated. A combination of filtration and chemical treatment is usually required to keep fog systems operational. Failure to properly evaluate water quality and treatment requirements before installation would be unwise.

Shade Systems

Fan and evaporative cooling systems are acceptable systems for greenhouse ventilation for some of the growing season. However, during the early fall planting season and the late spring harvest period, additional measures are needed to control excess heat build-up in the greenhouse.

Excess heat (above 85°F) can contribute to several growth and fruit ripening problems. During these periods, when the radiation load on the greenhouse exceeds what the evaporative cooling system can handle, shading of the plants is needed.

There are basically two approaches: shade paint and shade cloths. The white shading compound is applied to the outside of the poly greenhouse cover. The shade cloths can be applied over the house or within the house on a trellis system.

HORIZONTAL AIR FLOW FANS

When the large ventilation fans are not operating, smaller horizontal air circulation fans can provide more uniform humidity, temperature, and CO_2 in the greenhouse to ensure more consistent performance by plants throughout the house. Air circulation can also minimize the formation of free water on plants to prevent the development of disease organisms, and can prevent condensation on the inner glazing surface.

INSTALLING POLY ROOF

After building your greenhouse you are ready to install your poly film. Two sheets are required. Each sheet is positioned in place, one on top of the other, and fastened down with 1"x 2"x 12' wood strips. Roll the excess on the board, pull tight, then nail to the top of the sides.

Now install a blower (squirrel cage type) that will inflate between the two layers, forming a 1' to 2' air pocket. These are made especially for greenhouses and can be purchased at your supply house. Directions are usually supplied with unit. The idea is to cut a hole approximately 2" square in the top 1"x 6"x 12'. Cut through the bottom layer of poly but not the top. Fasten the bottom layer around the hole with wood and screws.

Adjustments can be made for more or less air in the roof by cutting another 3" square hole at the other end and using one screw to fasten a 4" square door on top of it, allowing it to be opened or closed. Try to maintain about 1½' of air at the middle and sides.

INFLATION KIT

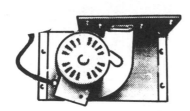

For inflating double layered houses.

- Keeps poly tight-helps control condensation.
- Compact-easy to use.
- All wiring and mounting brackets built-in.
- Built-in damper.

Poly films are made in different qualities. Some (cheaper ones) may last one or two years, whereas the better ones can last four years or longer. They may cost twice as much, but they can save a lot of time and money in reduced labor and replacement costs.

Covering end walls can be as simple as stapling poly to the outside using webbing strips available at supply houses. In cold weather put an extra layer on the end side to form a 4" dead space and greatly improve heating. Sides can be made of roll-up curtains (available from Speedling Inc., Sun City, Florida), or double poly with a 3" hose supplying air from roof. A faster, cheaper way is to purchase poly film a few feet wider (approximately 8'); roll ends and staple to frame. One layer will be fine if no high winds are expected.

POLY-FILM

Size			Approx. Cost
4 Mil Size	***Fold**	**Wt./ Roll**	**Price 1 - 4**
24' x 100'	C	58 lbs.	$92.25
32' x 100'	G	71 lbs.	$122.95
40' x 100'	G	91 lbs.	$153.75
40' x 150'	G	131 lbs.	$230.75
14'4" x 220'	G	141 lbs.	$242.50
6 Mil Size	***Fold**	**Wt./ Roll**	**Price 1 - 4**
14' x 100'	C	45 lbs.	$80.75
16' x 100'	C	51 lbs.	$92.25
20' x 100'	C	68 lbs.	$115.50
24' x 100'	C	81 lbs.	$138.50
28' x 100'	C	91 lbs.	$161.50
32' x 100'	G	101 lbs.	$184.50
32' x 110'	G	110 lbs.	$202.95
32' x 150'	G	150 lbs.	$276.75
40' x 100'	G	130 lbs.	$230.75
40' x 110'	G	141 lbs.	$253.75
40' x 150'	G	188 lbs.	$345.95
42' x 100'	G	131 lbs.	$242.25
48' x 100'	G	156 lbs.	$290.50
20' x 110'	GT	140 lbs.	$253.75
20' x 150'	GT	190 lbs.	$345.95
24' x 100'	GT	156 lbs.	$290.75
24' x 150'	GT	226 lbs.	$435.95

C=Centerfold, G=Gusseted, GT=Gusseted Tube

BASIC PLANS FOR 30'x 96' SOLAR GREENHOUSE

MATERIAL LIST:

Pressure Treated Lumber

34	8' x 4" x 4"	Side Posts
17	14' x 4" x 4"	Middle Posts
32	12' x 1" x 6"	Ridge Bars, Ground Plates
40	16' x 2" x 4"	Rafters and End Plates
80	12' x 2" x 4"	Braces, Sides, Rafter Braces, Rafter Ends
16	12' x 1" x 4"	Upper Braces
20	8' x 2" x 4"	End Studs, Braces
16	12' x 2" x 4"	Side Post Rafter Seats
24	12' x 1" x 2"	Securing Poly Roof
2	4' x 8' x ⅝"	Plywood

Galvanized Nails
50 Lbs 16p
25 Lbs 10p

Poly-Film
40'x 100' 6 mil 2 rolls
Patching Tape 1 roll

Blower Fan and Wiring

CONSTRUCTION STEPS:

STEP 1: Set **17 8' x 4" x 4"s** 1½' in ground, 6' apart on each side. Total 34. Set **17 14' x 4" x 4"s** down the middle of greenhouse, 6' apart from center of post to center of post. Set 3½' in ground.

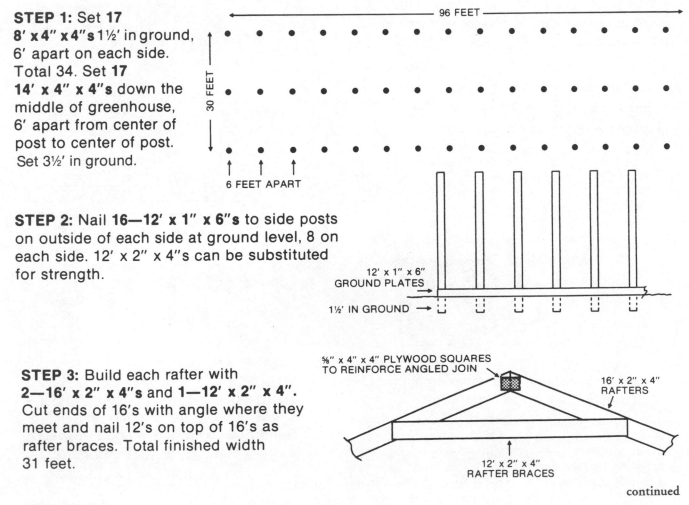

STEP 2: Nail **16—12' x 1" x 6"s** to side posts on outside of each side at ground level, 8 on each side. 12' x 2" x 4"s can be substituted for strength.

STEP 3: Build each rafter with **2—16' x 2" x 4"s** and **1—12' x 2" x 4"**. Cut ends of 16's with angle where they meet and nail 12's on top of 16's as rafter braces. Total finished width 31 feet.

continued

BASIC PLANS FOR 30'x 96' SOLAR GREENHOUSE
(continued)

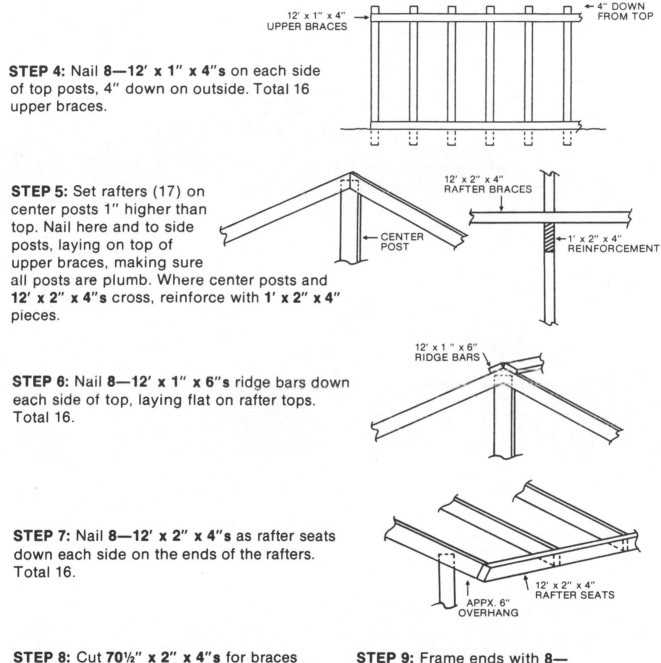

12' x 1" x 4"
UPPER BRACES

← 4" DOWN
FROM TOP

STEP 4: Nail **8—12' x 1" x 4"s** on each side of top posts, 4" down on outside. Total 16 upper braces.

STEP 5: Set rafters (17) on center posts 1" higher than top. Nail here and to side posts, laying on top of upper braces, making sure all posts are plumb. Where center posts and **12' x 2" x 4"s** cross, reinforce with **1' x 2" x 4"** pieces.

12' x 2" x 4"
RAFTER BRACES

← CENTER
POST

1' x 2" x 4"
REINFORCEMENT

STEP 6: Nail **8—12' x 1" x 6"s** ridge bars down each side of top, laying flat on rafter tops. Total 16.

12' x 1" x 6"
RIDGE BARS

STEP 7: Nail **8—12' x 2" x 4"s** as rafter seats down each side on the ends of the rafters. Total 16.

12' x 2" x 4"
RAFTER SEATS

APPX. 6"
OVERHANG

STEP 8: Cut **70½" x 2" x 4"s** for braces between rafters, two between each rafter. Total 64. See large illustration.

STEP 9: Frame ends with **8— 16' x 2" x 4"s** (2 upper braces and 2 end ground plates each side), and **7— 8' x 2" x 4"** studs for each end. Build door with ⅝" plywood between 2 end studs. See large illustration.

®1990 T.M. TAYLOR CO.

(To build 30' x 48' greenhouse, divide materials in half and build according to instructions.)

continued

BASIC PLANS FOR 30'x 96' SOLAR GREENHOUSE
(continued)

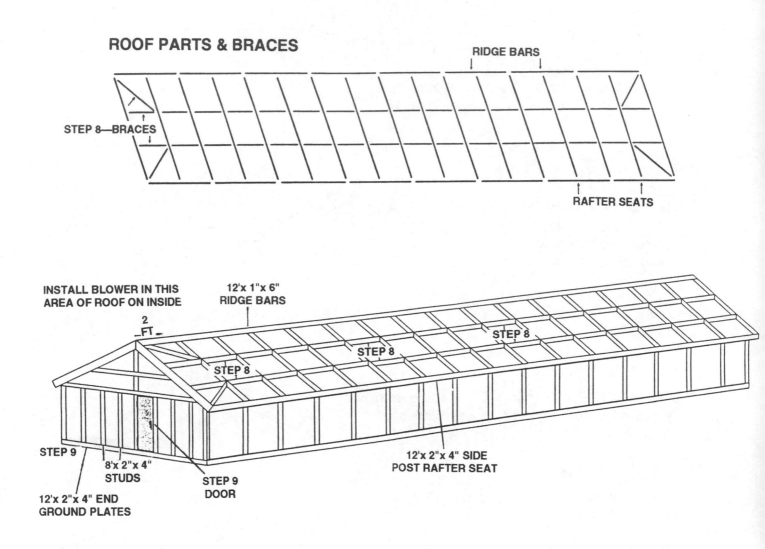

ROOF PARTS & BRACES

RIDGE BARS

STEP 8—BRACES

RAFTER SEATS

INSTALL BLOWER IN THIS
AREA OF ROOF ON INSIDE

12'x 1"x 6"
RIDGE BARS

2
FT

STEP 8

STEP 8

STEP 8

STEP 8

STEP 9

8'x 2"x 4"
STUDS

STEP 9
DOOR

12'x 2"x 4" END
GROUND PLATES

12'x 2"x 4" SIDE
POST RAFTER SEAT

STEP 10: Pull one roll of Poly-Film
6 mil over each side of greenhouse roof using
ropes. Tie all corners down. After both sheets
are even, use double-headed nails and
12'x 1" x 2"s, rolling the ends under and
nailing to the side post rafter seat.

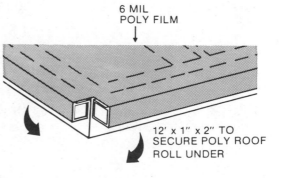

6 MIL
POLY FILM

12' x 1" x 2" TO
SECURE POLY ROOF
ROLL UNDER

Section 4

Selling, Marketing, and Economics

When beginning a greenhouse business a lot of your time will be spent advertising and promoting your plants. Hopefully you will have some idea of who you are going to sell to. Make a written outline of the steps you will take: from talking with interested buyers to planting seasonal crops, advertising, purchasing boxes and sleeves, and arranging delivery.

Some people are more comfortable letting a broker do all the selling while they put their own attention on the technical aspects of growing plants. Others enjoy the excitement of closing a large deal on regular truckload deliveries. Management and problem-solving skills are very important at this point.

SALES CONCEPTS

The most important rule in the plant business is: *Never sell anything you are not completely satisfied with.* Sell only items that are healthy, top quality, and balanced with the cost.

Be proud of what you grow and grow proud; you are doing a great service for Mother Earth. With the greenhouse effect people are more aware of the importance of planting. You will be admired for your participation in this work.

If selling retail, promote the idea that your customers can use plants to purify the air in their homes. Boron levels, which can be harmful, may be reduced to a safe atmosphere with just a few houseplants.

Most areas of the plant industry will continue to grow and prosper because of increasing awareness of the importance of sound ecology. Use this to your benefit in every way.

Some varieties of fast-growing trees can be effectively promoted to wholesale buyers using an environmental approach. Suggest that they advertise with an ecology overtone and the results will be astounding.

The appearance of your business is important when buyers come out to see you. A well-maintained nursery will give your customers the impression of success.

THE TELEPHONE — AN IMPORTANT TOOL

A wholesaler's primary sales tool is usually the telephone. An 800 number will increase out-of-state business and is suggested.

The telephone is the next best thing to being there. In many cases you will find the phone *is* better than being there. By using the phone you can project the image you want without worrying about what you look like. Research has shown that difficult customers are sometimes better handled by phone. You're more able to ask frank questions that you might hesitate to ask in person. It's also a lot easier to ask for a large order over the phone than in person. Asking for a yes or no is a much simpler matter, and prospects are more inclined not to second-guess like sometimes happens at sit-down meetings.

Try to make your appeal stand out from the rest of the pack. When selling, use a casual language that sounds the same way you talk. Though not always grammatically correct, this will make prospects feel that you are sincere and spontaneous. For instance, "How ya doin?" instead of the more formal "How are you?" can sound more genuine.

The ideal telephone sales call should be about four minutes. Be snappy and graphic; get to the point.

Telephone sales usually have four phases:

Opener

Description

Close

Confirmation

The beginning of the call is a crucial time, during which the relationship in the conversation is forged. Notice the tone of voice that another uses at the beginning of a call. If some-one sounds down you can often pull them out of the blues by contrasting your voice with theirs. Accomplish this by making your tone go up at the end of certain words and lines. For example, instead of saying flatly "Hello Sara," phrase the greeting as a question: "Hello Sara?" This will enliven your voice and most likely will do the same for your prospect.

Convey a positive attitude toward the person you call: a cheerful, friendly, confident attitude that reflects a genuine interest in the other person. Prepare some questions to ask and write them down. Gather material and data you may need before you call. Unless your voice is instantly recognized, identify yourself to the buyer. Ask if they have time to talk now. Come to the point as quickly as possible; do not needlessly prolong the conversation. A lot of orders can be taken over the phone without the buyer ever seeing the plants if you can show that you're sincere and enthusiastic, and you can accurately describe the size and color of your product.

The person who initiates the phone call is usually the one who should end the conversation. (Some large companies have a policy of waiting for the customer to end the conversation.) You may guide the call to a conclusion by saying "I'm sorry, but I'm late for an appointment" or "It sure was nice of you to call."

Two positive qualities you can project are friendliness and consideration. To project friendliness, use a warm, cordial tone and manner. Be attentive and responsive to your buyer. Appearing considerate is mainly a matter of listening to the other person's reactions and responding on them. This way you show them that you understand their point of view.

To show your sincerity, keep your voice clear, your inflection up, and your tone bright and natural. Relate what you say to the needs and viewpoint of the other person. Avoid extravagant claims and exaggerations.

Phone sales are generally made with a verbal agreement. (When the plants are delivered, they are inspected to check on specifications.) You may want to send a sample to your buyer, at which time you can also send a purchase order. Always follow up with important buyers by sending a sample, even if they have shown little or no interest. It is easier for the buyer to say no over the phone than in person. Remember, most large buyers can never find enough high quality plants. To encourage both large and small buyers you may want to leave a dozen or so plants to be sold. This will let the buyer see what amount she would want to purchase.

Selling can be easy when done properly. Getting an important buyer can be troublesome and can cost many hard-earned dollars, or it can be easy and almost cost-free if done a particular way. There is almost no buyer that can resist your product if you present it correctly. You must have a high quality product and spend your time selling the top grade of the plants. These are difficult for buyers to find and will bring a handsome profit for you in time. Large buyers are where the money is, so if you plan to make a good profit start at the top. There are usually three to ten good market outlets in every state. These include department stores, grocers, restaurant chains, open markets, brokers, truckers, and flower wholesale houses.

PICKING THE RIGHT MARKET

In your basic marketing study look carefully at the segment of the market you want to hone in on. The days of sending your plants to a traditional wholesaler and hoping for the best are gone forever.

Your first decision is: Will your outlet be a florist, discount chain (Walmart/K-Mart), grocery chain, or garden center? Each has its own personality.

❖ RETAIL FLORISTS. Most sales come in by phone. Most product moves out on the florist delivery truck. Interesting: Florists control 90% of what goes out their door. Their consumers have very little choice. If the owner doesn't like red flowers, you won't see many in his shop.

❖ DISCOUNT CHAINS. Walmart/K-Mart types are mostly looking for low prices and reasonable quality. To meet this intense price competition, you must go to high-density production and make other concessions. If this is the market you decide to sell to, you must close your eyes to many things such as quality and prompt payment.

❖ GARDEN CENTERS. A special breed, garden centers are like the retail florists in some ways, but they do a lot more cash and carry. They are also one of the fastest growing outlets for foliage plants (not many centers grow their own).

❖ GROCERY CHAINS. A little different style. We have found in our marketing studies that the grocery chain buyer is interested in diverse pot sizes. They sell from 4" to 4' trees. Many of these markets today have full service floral shops from 500 to 1,500 square feet. Many operate like florists, offering full service for weddings and funerals.

Their biggest asset is that the homemaker pops into the supermarket an average of two times per week. In other words, they have very high traffic. If the grocery chain is your target, you will find demand for:

❖ 4½" pot, in high demand
❖ 5½", very strong demand
❖ 6" and 6½", also very high sales
❖ 8" and 10" hanging baskets
❖ quality wanted: good to excellent

Supermarket buyers rate their suppliers on: (1) quality of product—most important, (2) service—next important, and (3) price—last!

MAKING THE SALES PRESENTATION

Leave Samples

Always leave a few samples wherever you go, even when contact was not made with the appropriate buyer. Sometimes a buyer will have to change plans at the last minute and reschedule the appointment. If you have traveled a considerable distance, let the secretary know this and ask if there is another buyer who can inspect your samples and pass on the price and information list.

Be sure to leave a new sample every time you visit. You might have to return to explain additional information or go over shipping plans. Bring new samples of other plants you want to sell. This is a good time to get the buyer's attention.

If the size of one group of plants varies significantly, take one of the largest and one of the smallest as samples, and explain that the rest will be in between the sizes shown. Never take any samples that are not top quality material.

Standing Orders

After getting your first order and making delivery, allow about 30 days and follow up with a request for a standing order: weekly, monthly, every other month, or a few times a year in the appropriate season for seasonal crops. After the date and variety have been decided on, agree on cancellation terms, if any, and get purchase order numbers (for the next shipment only). Standing orders might take as long as six to twelve months to arrange with the larger buyers, but they are worth every minute of the time you spend dealing with their procedures.

Offer Plant Promotions

Be creative! A surefire method of getting your plants in a particular store is to offer a plant promotion package. This package may contain any of the following: Offer, say, 100 or more plants at your truckload price. Put them in one store to test the amount of sales they will generate. The secret is to have one type (or two at the most), and make sure it is a top seller for your area. Have them all displayed at the same time, and make an agreement that the buyer may buy only the ones he has sold after one month if he likes. You may want to make the time period shorter or longer. In any case, use as many plants as possible. Keep daily records of sales, and clean up plants if needed to promote larger sales.

Ask the buyer to include the promotion along with food items in his weekly newspaper ads. Ask for display space around the front of store. Plant tables can be made by turning shipping boxes upside down and using pyramid-style stacking. Cover with plants and you have one of the best displays you can make.

Use pricing that inspires volume purchases (like $6 each or 2 for $10; 2 for $1 or 3 for $5). This kind of pricing strategy usually increases sales greatly. Once the buyer sees the profits from your package he will happily place another order. Remember, there is always a demand for healthy, top quality plants. Buyers cannot find enough nurseries to supply top grade all the time, and so they will occasionally sell plants of lower quality. This is when the creative grower will become the creative seller and offer a higher quality plant.

Sell the sizzle, not the steak (size, color, quality, fast delivery, quick sell, etc.). Make your first presentation short and make every word count. The first ten words are more important than the next thousand. Talk about the plant, then prove it. Use showmanship and professional mannerisms. Mention that you are the best, the biggest, or the only one doing it. Show confidence.

Your largest nearby department or grocery store is a good place to start. Get a feel for the plant types and quantities they buy by contacting their store manager or produce buyer. Tell him you have started a plant nursery. Ask how often he receives shipments, what types and quantities of plants he buys, and whether he feels he is getting top quality plants. Be very friendly. Be sure to thank him for his time.

Then go home with this information and call the main district buyer for the store you have checked. Tell him who you are, that you have a wholesale plant nursery, and that you stopped by one of his stores and saw the manager. For instance, if the store you visited had difficulty getting pothos, tell him you are interested in growing assorted plants and plan to grow pothos; would he be interested in buying them? If so, tell him you will get back with him about packing information, and that you will send him a sample. Find out how many stores he would be buying for, and the amount he usually orders of that variety.

Try a few stores and find out if any are alike. For instance, do all the stores need the same thing? (Usually they do.) This is where you fill the gap, your first opportunity. Grow some (perhaps 500) of the variety of your choice. When grown take about 20 or so and clean up the pots. Then put them in a couple of plant boxes and go off to show them.

Make an appointment with the store buyer. Be prepared with:

Price list
Care tag information
Packing information
Delivery date
Payment terms

Be prompt for the appointment! Walk in the office and set a couple of plants on the buyer's desk. Say "Good morning (or afternoon) Mr. or Ms. _____. Aren't these mighty nice or the nicest looking plants?

"I've grown them myself and I'm willing to give you a good deal on them. I will give you the truckload price on the first 1,000 plants (truckloads are usually about 5,000 in the 4" pot) for you to use as samples and try out. Larger orders will have to be 200 or 350 boxes (40' truckload) to get this price."

After hearing this, if she is interested she will want to know your regular price (about 10% more), which makes the large quantity order look good.

You have her attention now. Tell her that you grow these plants in a weed-free soil, that you clean all pots before shipment, that you guarantee the plants will be a certain size when delivered, and that quality will never fall below this.

The seed, cutting, or plantlet will probably be the cheapest part of the planted pot, so put one or two extra in a pot for fast results. This reduces the time it takes to produce a salable plant and is one of the best selling points you will have. Tell the buyer how they are grown, what type of fertilizer you use, and if you have them protected from the weather. (This will assure her you can make prompt deliveries.)

If she says she doesn't have room, suggest a plant promotional project, setting the plants next to counters, on windowsills, or hanging them up. If the price seems high to her, ask what she is paying for this size and type of plant, and beat it if you can. You can always come up on the price in a couple of months, when she sees that your plants will sell and she can count on you.

Get the first and every order on paper if possible.

USING VIDEOTAPE

A very useful tool for promoting your plants is a video camcorder. With a little practice, you can make a quality tape. Camcorders can be rented from most tape rental stores if you don't own one.

Make duplicate VCR recorded tapes from the original camera tape at a cost of only a couple of dollars each. Send one to each buyer who might be interested in your plants or vegetables. This will be the cheapest sales call you can make, and probably the most cost effective!

You may also want to send tapes out a couple of weeks before your crop is ready to sell. Your buyers then have an opportunity to see the quality and value of your crop before they have taken steps to purchase someone else's crop.

Most buyers seem to enjoy watching tapes of plants that interest them. The video is entertaining as well as a great sales tool. Very few growers are using this excellent media.

Your tape should describe some of the more technical aspects of your business, number of employees, types of plants produced, delivery, and methods of growing. You might also mention any large buyers that you sell to. A ten-minute tape is long enough for your visual tour.

Try to give the potential buyer the idea that you are offering quality, consistency, and a clean plant. Remember, *"A picture is worth a thousand words."*

At trade shows you will find the video a real crowd stopper. This is that something extra that others might not have.

MAKING YOUR VIDEO

First, design guidelines on what scenes will be shot and what your "voiceover" will say. Second, escort the film crew to the most significant aspects of your business, showing them what to shoot. Videos will be more effective than flyers or brochures simply because they use sound and motion. The audience will be "locked in" for ten minutes. So be sure to get your point across. It should be the next best thing to being there, like the buyer taking a tour in person.

Videos should not replace print advertising. They should be part of a complete, well-rounded promotion program. They should entice your buyers to place more and larger orders by conveying a good impression of your business.

The most valuable aspect of videotapes is to get others to view and perceive your nursery the way you do. All the extra touches you can add to make your tape exciting will be worth the time and expense.

USING A MAILING LIST

There are over 140,000 grocery stores in the United States. The major ones can usually be dealt with by calling one person. The others can be notified efficiently using a purchased mailing list. Names are sold by the thousand (usually between $50 and $100 per thousand). You can get them for a particular area or by size. The library will have a copy of *Direct Mail List Rates and Date,* or for $92 you can order this semi-annual book from Standard Rate & Data Service, 5201 Old Orchard Rd, Skokie, IL, 60076.

There are over 11,000 health food stores and 25,000 department stores which can be located through your yellow pages. Listed on the next page are the number of businesses found in the yellow pages. Details on these businesses can be obtained from: American Business List, 5711 South 86th Circle, P.O. Box 27347, Omaha, Nebraska 68127, (402) 331-7169, FAX (402) 331-1505.

POTENTIAL PLANT BUYERS	# OF BUSINESSES
Department Stores	25,449
Discount Stores	1,106
Florist - Retail	49,739
Flower Growers & Shippers	312
Fruit & Vegetables - Brokers	502
Fruit & Vegetables - Retail	9,202
Fruit & Vegetables - Wholesale	1,716
Gardeners	18,232
Garden Centers	5,252
Groceries - Retail	140,892
Health Food Stores	11,745
Herbs - Retail	1,496
Landscape Contractors	32,145
Lawn & Garden Supplies	11,653
Nurseryman's Equipment & Supplies	533
Plants - Interior Renting & Leasing	532
Plants - Retail	11,153
Plants - Wholesale	1,106

BROCHURES

Perhaps the most common direct mail promotion is the letter package. It consists of a letter (from one to twelve pages long), business reply envelope, order form, and brochure. This kind of promotion has proven successful time and time again.

To create an effective brochure:

❖ Describe the complete offer, so if the brochure gets separated from the rest of the mailing package the buyer can still order.

❖ Put the main selling message on the front cover. Most buyers will not read past the cover if it does not grab their interest.

❖ Two or more colors almost always get better results than a single-color brochure.

❖ "Lift letters" are short letters that supplement the sales pitch laid out in the longer full-size letter. They can be printed on half-sheets or smaller pieces of paper. When prepared effectively, they can greatly increase results.

FLYERS/SELF-MAILERS

These are mailing formats that do not require an envelope. Designs range from simple folded leaflets to large folded brochures printed on card stock. Self-mailers offer several advantages:

❖ They save money because they require no outside envelope.

❖ They save time because you don't have to stuff them in envelopes.

❖ They are generally quick and easy to design and produce.

A really fast way to promote your plants is to send flyers to the main and secondary buyers. Anyone who handles a large volume of business should be contacted (plant brokers, department stores, retail nurseries, home builder supply stores, and grocery chains).

Flyers can be made quickly and easily using laser color copying and your letterhead. You may want to use stencils, obtained at any bookstore, to create a more professional look. Put only the most important information on the flyer—do not crowd it. List the type of plant, size, pot size, price in quantity, plants per box, size of box, plants per pot, average height and width of plant, and quantity available. Include delivery requirements and payment terms (such as 2% discount if paid in ten days, 30-day finance charge, C.O.D.). Cash on delivery should always be stressed until good working relations and credit have been established. Be competitive when deciding how much to charge per plant. Quantity discounts are entirely up to you. If you have plenty of buyers, stay firm on your price. But if you want to get fast action just drop your price by 10 or 15¢ each. Be sure to stress how large, full, clean, healthy, and reasonable your plants are.

Don't think that by selling your plants at a lower rate you won't make as much money. I have found the opposite to be true. Usually you get lots of business you never counted on. Price increases every six months are common.

CREATIVE SELLING: THE COMPETITIVE EDGE

An important ingredient in a successful retail or wholesale business is good selling. Without it, many sales are lost—sales that can mean the difference between success and failure. Train yourself and your employees to become creative salespeople.

To many customers, the salesperson is the business. Therefore, if the salespeople are good, the business is good. But if the salespeople are poor, it greatly impacts the business. Although important to all businesses, effective salespeople are especially important to small businesses. While it may be difficult for a small business to compete with the big firms on things like assortment, price, and promotion, selling effort is one place where the wholesale grower or service retail business can compete with larger competitors—and win.

Effective selling doesn't happen by accident. The small entrepreneur must work to achieve a high level of sales effectiveness in his or her business. In order to work toward this goal, the businessperson should be aware of the different types of salespeople, the selling process, and the attributes of effective salespeople. Applying this knowledge to a business situation should result in a competitive edge.

TYPES OF SALESPEOPLE

There are three main types of sales personnel:

1. ORDER-HANDLER. The truckdriver making deliveries, the checker at the retail nursery—these salespeople are working in a routine selling environment. Due to the nature of their jobs, they will be asked numerous questions and hear complaints about prices and service from customers. A knowledgeable person with a pleasant personality is especially needed for this job, because this is usually the person who is dealing with the customer when the customer's money is received.

2. ORDER-TAKER. More creativity is found in this job compared to the order-handler. The counter attendant at the nursery may take the order and then suggest that the customer might also wish to buy a new variety. Pleasant personality, fast service, and suggestion selling on the part of the order-taker can result in many additional sales.

3. ORDER-GETTER. For many businesses, the heart of the selling process rests with the creative selling efforts of their salespeople. Of course, one of the greatest problems is that there are order-handlers and order-takers in many selling positions that should be staffed by order-getters for optimum selling effectiveness. A person who can handle a transaction, take an order, and, most importantly, get an order should be used. Even though all selling situations do not call for order-getters, all salespeople will be called upon to sell creatively from time to time. It is for this reason that all salespeople need to have a working knowledge of the creative selling process.

CREATIVE SELLING PROCESS

The creative selling process consists of eight steps. No step is less important than any other if the process is to be effective. Emphasize to all employees that every step is vital to effective selling.

1. *Pre-Customer Contact*

A smart builder would not attempt to build a house without a good foundation. Likewise, you should not place people on the sales floor or telephone until they know the business, merchandise, services, and customers. Before any contact is made with the customer, a salesperson should know:

POLICIES, PROCEDURES, AND RULES. Have these in writing, accessible to all employees.

TARGET MARKET KNOWLEDGE. The best salespeople know something about the likes and dislikes of the firm's primary customers. The business operator should tell all salespeople about the business's customers: lifestyles, interests, and ability to buy.

PRODUCT KNOWLEDGE. A salesperson gains confidence by knowing about the products and services s/he is selling. Some salespeople will not take the initiative to acquire plant knowledge on their own. It is management's responsibility to encourage employees to gain product and service knowledge. Management should make such knowledge available to them.

2. *Prospecting*

Although not appropriate to every selling situation, prospecting should be used whenever possible. Essentially, prospecting means not waiting for the customer to show up or phone the nursery to inquire about a service. Prospecting means taking the initiative by going to the customer with a plant or service idea. There are two types: new or regular customer prospecting.

NEW CUSTOMER PROSPECTING. A salesperson sees that an opportunity exists. Action is taken on this knowledge by contacting the prospect and telling them about appropriate items that you have. By using sales lists, yellow pages, and personal contacts, a salesperson can take the initiative to contact and create new customers.

REGULAR CUSTOMER PROSPECTING. A firm's best prospects are its current customers. A salesperson should call regular customers periodically to tell them about plants or services. Prospecting with regular customers works! Salespeople should be encouraged to prospect by phone and in person whenever they see regular customers. A word of caution here: Don't go to the well too often. Prospecting with a regular customer too frequently can take away from the customer's feeling that this is a special opportunity. Do not overuse it.

3. *Initial Contact*

The most effective way to close a sale is to open it on a positive note. Also, because the customer has heard the statement many times, their response is usually given automatically without thinking about what was said. Salespeople should treat each customer as an individual and respond differently to each one.

PRESENTATION OF PLANTS. In presenting plants to the buyer, the salesperson should use plant knowledge to best advantage. Here are some techniques to do so:

BUYER BENEFITS. Although it is good to talk about the plants' growing conditions, customers will probably be more interested in hearing about how many and how often you can supply them. Plant knowledge is important, but the salesperson must remember what makes the customer buy. Sell benefits! For example, if your plastic pots are top grade plastic, the important benefit is that they will not break under normal shipping and handling.

BUYER INVOLVEMENT. Plant knowledge can be used to get a buyer's involvement. Show the buyer a couple of different store promotion plans at your expense or his, on credit or cash up front. The best way to present many plants is to get buyer involvement.

Be sure to leave samples for his office and the secretary's office.

LIMIT THE CHOICES. If you present more than three different types of plants to the buyer, the chance of a sale is reduced unless there is a definite reason for an exception. Presenting limited choices is a proven way to increase sales.

4. *Showmanship*

In presenting plants to the buyer, encourage all personnel to be creative. Be enthusiastic about the quality. Ask your salespeople to think like a customer. If I were a customer, what would I want to see? Be knowledgeable about things such as how much light is needed for healthy growth? How long will plants survive in a box without light during shipping? Will they bruise easily? Are herbs organically grown? Any questions that you can think of your buyer will probably think of too. Be ready and sure of yourself. Point out relevant facts: that you use sterile soil, care tags, or slow-release fertilizer that lasts for three months, or that you guarantee no insect damage.

MESSAGE ADAPTATION. A good salesperson will decide what information should be presented to a specific customer. "Canned" sales presentations do not allow for adaptation. An effective salesperson will adjust the presentation to the knowledge and interests of the customer. If the customer knows about gardens and lawns, the person selling a lawn service should adapt the sales presentation to the level of that customer's expertise. Don't bore the customer with known facts. It could lose a sale.

5. *Handling Objections*

If objections are present, progress is probably being made on the sale. Most salespeople are afraid of objections. Stress to employees that objections are a natural part of the selling process. They do not mean that the sale is lost. An objection usually just means that the customer needs more information. All that is required is more selling by the salesperson.

6. *Closing the Sale*

In various ways, the salesperson can assist the customer by helping them make the buying decision. Closing techniques that can aid in this effort include:

OFFER A SERVICE. *"Let us deliver it to you this afternoon."* A "yes" implies purchase.

GIVE A CHOICE. *"Do you want five or eight?"* Either choice implies purchase. Note that "no" is not one of the choices.

OFFER AN INCENTIVE. *"If you buy now, you get 10% off the already low price."* If you wait you don't get the 10% discount.

BETTER NOT WAIT. *"If you want this load, better get it now. It's the last one."* Note, it pays to be honest. If the customer buys and then comes in the next day and sees that you have another load, this closing technique could make a sale but lose a customer.

7. *Suggestion Selling*

Encourage your salespeople to make a definite suggestion for a possible additional sale. For many businesses, sales can be increased by 25% through creative suggestion selling. Where appropriate, the salesperson should actually get the suggested item and show it to the customer. This type of initiative usually results in more sales. It should be emphasized that most customers *appreciate* receiving a valid suggestion. Good suggestion selling makes sales and builds confidence in the firm's business.

8. *Sales Follow-Up*

Although not apparent to many salespeople, follow-up is a part of every sale. Follow-up may include checking on anything that was promised to the buyer as part of the sale. For example, if delivery is supposed to take place on Friday, the salesperson might check to make sure the promise will be met and, if it won't, notify the buyer of the problem. Good sales follow-up will prevent the type of situation that often occurs when the customer calls on Friday asking, "Where is the delivery truck?"

Sincere sales follow-up is good business practice. It builds goodwill, and a company with a reputation for good sales follow-up will receive repeat business.

ATTRIBUTES OF A CREATIVE SALESPERSON

In addition to having personnel who understand and regularly apply the creative selling process, an organization needs salespeople who possess certain attributes that can make them more effective in their jobs. These attributes can be grouped into mental and physical categories.

JUDGMENT. Good judgment, common sense, maturity, intelligence—these terms are all ways of saying: *Respect your buyer's opinions and desires.* A good salesperson knows it does not pay to argue with a buyer. This is good judgment on the part of the employee. The term maturity is sometimes used in place of judgment, but it is not necessarily a function of age. Many older people do not use good judgment, while some young employees have a high level of common sense.

ATTITUDE. A good salesperson will have a positive attitude toward customers, merchandise, services, and the business. A good attitude means that an employee is willing to accept suggestions, learn and apply the steps in the creative selling process, and is not afraid of work. A salesperson with a poor attitude can create unnecessary problems. A bad attitude is contagious. If such an employee is otherwise competent, management should work with the employee to develop a positive attitude. Positive attitudes can result in sales.

SELECTED PHYSICAL ATTRIBUTES. To be a success, the salesperson must physically belong in the firm's particular environment. Personal appearance and hygiene are important in the selling environment. Personal appearance *does* count in the selling equation.

A business can greatly enhance its probability of success by stressing the creative selling process and giving special attention to the desired mental and physical attributes of a salesperson. Good creative selling can provide the competitive edge.

PLAN YOUR ADVERTISING BUDGET

Deciding how much your advertising to do, how much to invest in increasing sales, and how that amount should be allocated is totally up to you, the small business owner. Advertising costs are a completely controllable expense. Advertising budgets are the means of determining and controlling this expense and dividing it wisely between departments, lines, or services.

This section describes various methods for intelligently establishing an advertising budget. Then it suggests ways to apply budget amounts for the results you want.

If you want to build sales, it's almost certain you'll need to advertise. How much should you spend? How should you allocate your advertising dollars? How can you be sure your advertising outlays aren't out of line? Your advertising budget helps you determine how much you will spend, and helps establish guidelines for how you will spend it.

What you'd like to invest in advertising and what you can afford are seldom the same. Spending too much can obviously be an extravagance, but spending too little can be just as bad in terms of lost sales and diminished visibility. Costs must be tied to results. You must be prepared to evaluate your goals and assess your capabilities; a budget will help you do precisely this.

Your budget will help you choose and assess the amount of advertising you will do, as well as its timing. It will also serve as background for next year's plan.

METHODS OF ESTABLISHING A BUDGET

Each of the methods of establishing an advertising budget has its drawbacks as well as its benefits. No method is perfect for all growers, nor for that matter is any combination of methods. The basic concepts from several traditional methods of budgeting have been combined into three basic methods. They are: (1) percentage of sales or profits, (2) unit of sales, and (3) objective and task. You'll need to use judgment and caution in deciding on your approach.

1. *Percentage of Sales or Profits*

The most widely used method of establishing an advertising budget is to base it on a percentage of sales. Advertising is as much a business expense as, say, the cost of labor, and thus should be related to the quantity of goods sold.

The percentage of sales method avoids some of the problems that result from using profits as a base. For instance, if profits in a period are low, it might not be the fault of sales or advertising. But if you stick with the same percentage figure, you'll automatically reduce your advertising allotment. There's no way around it: 2% of $10,000 is less than 2% of $15,000.

Such a cut in the advertising budget, if profits are down for other reasons, may very well lead to further reductions in advertising investment and so on.

In the short run a small greenhouse owner might make small additions to profit by cutting advertising expenses, but such a policy could lead to a long-term deterioration of the bottom line. By using the percentage of sales method, you keep your advertising in consistent relationship with your sales volume—which is what your advertising should be primarily affecting. Gross margin should also show an increase of course, especially over the long run, if your advertising outlays are being properly applied.

WHAT PERCENTAGE? You can guide your choice of a percentage of sales figure by finding out what other businesses like yours are doing. These percentages are generally consistent within a given category of business.

It's fairly easy to find out the ratio of advertising expense-to-sales in your business. Check trade magazines and associations. You can also find these percentages in census and Internal Revenue Service reports, and in reports published by financial institutions such as Dunn & Bradstreet, the Robert Morris Associates, and the Account Corporation of America.

Knowing what the ratio for your company is will help assure you that you are spending proportionately as much or more than your competitors. But remember, these industry averages are not gospel. Your particular situation may dictate that you want to advertise more or less than your competition. Average may not be good enough for you. You may want to "out-advertise" your competitors, and you may be willing to cut into short-term profits to do so. Growth takes investment.

No business owner should let any method bind him or her. It's helpful to use the percentage of sales method because it's quick and easy. It ensures that your advertising budget isn't way out of proportion for your business. It's a sound method for stable markets.

WHICH SALES? Your budget can be determined as a percentage of past sales, estimated future sales, or a combination of the two.

❖ *Past Sales:* Your base can be last year's sales or an average of a number of years in the immediate past. Consider, though, that changes in economic conditions can make your figure too high or low.

❖ *Estimated Future Sales:* You can calculate your advertising budget as a percentage of anticipated sales for the next year. The most common pitfall of this method is an optimistic assumption that your business will continue to grow. You must always keep general business trends in mind, especially if there's the chance of a slump, and hard-headedly assess the direction of your industry and your own operation.

❖ *Past Sales and Estimated Future Sales:* The middle ground between an often conservative appraisal based on last year's sales and a commonly overoptimistic assessment of next year's sales is to combine both methods. It's a more realistic approach during periods of changing economic conditions. It allows you to analyze trends and results thoughtfully and predict with more accuracy.

2. *Unit of Sales*

In the unit of sales method you set aside a fixed sum for each unit of product to be sold based on your experience and trade knowledge of how much advertising it takes to sell each unit. For example, if it takes two cents' worth of

advertising to sell one plant and you want to sell 10,000, you'll plan to spend $200 advertising them. Does it cost X dollars to sell a box full? Then you'll budget 1,000 times X if you plan to sell a thousand boxes full. You're basing your budget on unit of sales rather than dollar amount of sales.

Some people consider this method simply a variation of percentage of sales. However, unit of sales probably lets you make a better estimate of what to spend for maximum effect, since it's based on what experience tells you it takes to sell an actual unit rather than an overall percentage of your gross sales estimate.

The unit of sales method is particularly useful when the amount of product available is limited by outside factors such as the weather's effect on crops. If that's the situation for your business, first estimate how many units or cases will be available to you. Then, advertise only as much as experience tells you is required to sell the product. Thus, if you have a pretty good idea of how many units will be available, you should have minimal waste in your advertising costs.

3. *Objective and Task*

The most difficult (and least used) method for determining an advertising budget is the objective and task approach. Yet it's the most accurate and best accomplishes what all budgets should:

❖ It relates the appropriation to the marketing task to be accomplished.

❖ It relates the advertising appropriation under usual conditions and in the long run to the volume of sales, so that profits and reserves will not be drained.

To establish your budget by this method, you need a coordinated marketing program with specific objectives based on a thorough survey of your markets and their potential.

While the percentage of sales or profits method first determines how much you'll spend without much consideration of what you want to accomplish, the task method establishes what you must do in order to meet your objectives. Only then do you calculate its cost.

Set specific objectives. For example, don't just say "increase sales," but specify "sell 25% more of Type X or Y by attracting the business of grocery stores." Then determine what media best reaches your target market and estimate how much it will cost to run the number and types of ads you think it will take to get that sales increase. Repeat this process for each of your objectives. When you total these costs, you have your projected budget.

Of course, you may find that you can't afford to advertise as much as you would like to. It's a good idea, therefore, to rank your objectives. As with the other methods, be prepared to change your plan to reflect reality and fit the resources you have available.

HOW TO ALLOCATE YOUR BUDGET

Once you have determined your advertising budget, decide how you'll allocate your advertising dollars. First, decide if you will do any institutional advertising or if you'll do strictly promotional advertising.

After you set aside an amount to build your image (if that's part of your plan for the year), then allocate your promotional advertising in any number of ways. Among the most common breakdowns are by:

Departmental budgets
Total budget
Calendar periods
Media
Sales areas

1. Departmental Budgets
The most common method of allocating advertising dollars is percent of sales. Those departments or product categories with the greatest sales volume receive the biggest share of the budget.

In a small nursery or when the plant varieties are limited, the same percentage can be used throughout. Otherwise, a good rule is to use the industry average for each crop.

By breaking down the budget by departments or products, those plants that require more promotion to stimulate sales can get their required advertising dollars. Your budget can be further divided into individual merchandise lines.

2. Total Budget
Your total budget may be the result of integrated departmental or product budgets. If your business has set an upper limit for advertising expense percentage, then your departmental budgets, which are based on different percentages of sales in each area, might be pared down.

In smaller businesses the total budget may be the only one established. It, too, should be divided into merchandise classifications for scheduling.

3. Calendar Periods
Most executives of small businesses usually plan their advertising on a monthly or even a weekly basis. Your budget, even if it's for a longer planning period, ought to also be calculated for these shorter periods. It will give you better control.

The percentage of sales method is also useful to determine how much money to allocate by time period. The standard practice is to match sales with advertising dollars. Thus, if February accounts for 5% of your sales, you might give it 5% of your budget.

You may want to adjust advertising allocations downward in some of your stronger sales months and boost the budget in some of your slower periods. This should be done only if you have reason to believe that a change in your advertising timing will improve slow sales (such as when your competition's sales trends differ markedly from yours).

4. Media

The amount of advertising that you place in each advertising medium (such as direct mail, newspapers, or radio) should be determined by past experience, industry practice, and ideas from media specialists. Normally it's wise to use the same sort of media your competitors use. That's most likely to be where your potential customers look and listen.

5. Sales Areas

You can target your advertising dollars to geographical areas where your customers already exist or you can try to stimulate new sales areas. It's wise to do the bulk of your advertising in established areas. Usually it's more costly to develop new markets than to maintain existing markets.

A FLEXIBLE BUDGET

Any combination of these methods may be employed in establishing your advertising budget. However you plan your budget, make it flexible, and stay open to adjusting it in response to changes in the marketplace.

The duration of your planning and budgeting period depends on the nature of your business. If you use short budgeting periods, you'll find that your advertising can be more flexible, and that you can change tactics to meet immediate trends.

To ensure advertising flexibility, set aside a contingency fund for special circumstances—the introduction of a new product, competitors' specials available in local media, or other unexpected situations.

Beware of your competitors' activities at all times. Don't blindly copy what they're doing, but analyze how their actions may affect your business and be prepared to act.

GETTING STARTED

Your first budget will be the most difficult to develop but it will be worth the effort. By your second business year you'll have a more factual basis for budgeting than you did before—based on the results of your advertising. Your plans will become more effective with each budget you develop.

RECORDKEEPING IN YOUR NURSERY BUSINESS

For a new business, experience clearly indicates that an adequate recordkeeping system increases the chance of survival and reduces the probability of early failure. Similarly, for an established business, a good recordkeeping system definitely increases the chance of staying in business and earning large profits.

How do accounting records decrease the chance of failure and increase the likelihood of staying in business and earning larger profits? This can best be understood by looking at some of the information a simple but effective system of records can furnish:

How much business (cash and credit) am I doing? How much is tied up in receivables?

How are my collections? What are my losses

from credit sales? Who owes me money? Who is delinquent? Should I continue to extend credit to delinquent accounts? How soon can I anticipate a return on my accounts receivable?

How much cash do I have on hand and in the bank? Does this agree with what the records tell me I should have, or is there a shortage? What is my investment in merchandise? How often do I turn over my inventory? Have I allowed my inventory to become obsolete?

How much merchandise did I take out of my nursery for personal or family use which affects my gross profit calculations?

How much do I owe my suppliers and other creditors? Have I received all of my outstanding credits for returned merchandise?

How much gross profit (margin) did I earn?

What were my expenses, including those not requiring cash outlays?

What is my weekly payroll? Do I have adequate payroll records to meet the requirements of Worker's Compensation, Wage and Hour Laws, Social Security, Unemployment Insurance, and withholding taxes?

How much net profit did I earn, and how much resultant income tax will I owe?

What is my capital; that is, of my total assets, how much would be left for me after paying my creditors in full?

Are my sales, expenses, profits, and capital showing improvement, or did I do better than this last year? How do I stand compared with two periods ago? Is my position about the same, improving, or deteriorating?

On what lines of goods or in what departments am I making a profit, breaking even, or losing money?

Am I taking full advantage of cash discounts for prompt payments? How do my discounts taken compare with my discounts lost?

How do the financial facts of my business compare with those of similar businesses?

REQUIREMENTS OF A GOOD SYSTEM

A good recordkeeping system must be:

Simple to use

Easy to understand

Reliable

Accurate

Consistent

Designed to provide information on a timely basis

There are several copyrighted systems providing simplified records, usually in a simple record book. These systems cover the basic records with complete instructions for their use. You can examine some of these systems at most office supply stores.

CASH OR ACCRUAL BASIS

A very small business such as a roadside stand will use the cash basis for bookkeeping. A larger, more complicated business no doubt will use the accrual basis. The dividing line between the cash basis and accrual basis might depend on whether or not credit is granted to customers and the amount of inventory required.

Accrual basis is defined as "a method of recording income and expenses, in which each item is reported as earned or incurred, without regard to when actual payments are received or made." Charge sales are immediately credited to Sales and charged to Accounts Receivable. When the bills are collected, the credit is to Accounts Receivable.

Accruals should also be made for expense items payable in the future, such as yearly or semi-annual interest on loans.

GENERAL BOOKS OF ACCOUNT

A business needs some form of journal. A journal is used to record all business transactions.

The following is a typical journal entry.

January 31, 1991	Debit	Credit
Interest Expense	$58.33	
Accrued Interest Payable		$58.33

To record January share of interest due on First National Bank loan. Principal Amount $10,000 @ 7% = $700.00. January share $58.33.

The information for each transaction or journal entry is derived from original source documents (copies of sales slips, cash register tapes, check stubs, purchase orders, etc.). In fact, copies of such transaction records are often used as the journal, each record being an entry.

General ledgers are kept to record transactions and balances of individual accounts (Assets, Liabilities, Capital, Sales, and Expenses). At the end of each fiscal year or accounting period, accounts are balanced and closed. Sales (Income) and Expense account balances are transferred to the Summary of Revenue and Expenses and are used in the Income Statement. The remaining Asset, Liability, and Capital accounts provide the figures for the Balance Sheet.

Avoid using too many accounts. Subdivide sales into enough categories to show a clear picture of the business. Use different expense accounts covering frequent or substantial expenditures, but avoid minute distinctions which will tend to confuse rather than clarify. Use Miscellaneous Expense for small, unrelated expense items.

DEPRECIATION

A charge to expenses should be made to cover depreciation of fixed assets other than land. The corresponding credits are to Accumulated Depreciation.

Fixed assets may be defined as items normally used for one year or longer, such as buildings, automotive equipment, tools, equipment, furniture, and fixtures. Smaller businesses will usually charge depreciation at the end of their fiscal year.

ACCOUNTS RECEIVABLE CONTROL

A few rules should be followed to keep accounts receivable current. First, be sure bills are prepared when goods are shipped or service is rendered, and mail them to correct addresses. Keep a close watch on larger accounts.

At the end of each month, "age" your accounts receivable. List accounts and enter amounts that are current, unpaid for 30 days, and 60 days and over. Find out exactly why all accounts 60 days and older are unpaid. Your system should help you collect these accounts.

Pay close attention to customers' complaints about bills. If a complaint is justified, propose an adjustment and reach an agreement with the customer. Do this promptly.

If a customer is delinquent, try to obtain a promise of payment on a definite date. If payment is not received on the date promised, ask the customer to explain why and get a new promise.

If you don't know a customer who asks for credit, use a simple form listing name, address, telephone number, place of employment, and bank and credit references. Make sure that credit is warranted before you grant it.

PAYROLL RECORDS

Yearly and quarterly reports of individual payroll payments must be made to State and Federal governments. Each individual employee receives a W-2 form at year-end showing total withholding payments made for the employee during the calendar year.

An employment card should be kept for each employee showing, among other things, social security number, name, address, phone number, and name and address of next of kin. Indicate whether the employee is married and the number of exemptions claimed. A W-4 form should also be on record.

A summary payroll record should be made each payday showing each employee name, employee number, rate of pay, hours worked, overtime hours, total pay, and deductions for FICA, withholding taxes, insurance, pension, and/or saving plans.

A separate sheet should also be kept for each employee. On this individual record, list the rate of pay, social security number, and so on. Enter amounts for each pay period, hours worked, gross pay, and deductions. At the end of each quarter add the amounts and balance. These forms provide the data you need for quarterly and annual reports.

PETTY CASH FUND

Use a petty cash fund to pay small amounts not covered by invoices. Cash a check for, say, $25, and place the funds in a box or drawer. When paying for items such as postage, freight, and bus fares, list the items on a printed form or a blank sheet. When the fund is nearly exhausted, summarize the items and cash another check for the exact amount expended to replenish the fund. At all times the cash in the box plus listed expenditures equals the amount of the fund.

LIST EQUIPMENT

Keep a careful list of permanent equipment used in the business. Include any items useful for a year or longer that are of significant value. Show date purchased, supplier, description of item, amount of purchase, and check number. If you own a lot of these items, keep separate lists for automotive equipment, tools and potting equipment, and furniture and fixtures. These records provide the basis for calculating depreciation and provide supporting data for fixed asset accounts.

INSURANCE RECORD

Most businesses have several types of insurance. List each policy showing type of coverage, name of insurer, effective dates (including expiration), and annual premium. Be sure all necessary types of coverage are obtained. Ask your insurance agent to analyze your coverage.

OUTSIDE ACCOUNTING SERVICES

Many small firms seem to have the potential for success. Yet too often they fail because of poor financial management. In achieving effective financial management, the services of a public accountant are helpful. An accountant can design records, set up ways to maintain them, draw off vital information, and help relate it to a profitable operation.

Bits of information flow into a small firm every day. As customers are served, information is generated about sales, cash, equipment, expenses, payroll, accounts payable, and accounts receivable. A system is necessary to capture these facts and figures. An accountant can help design such a system to record the information an owner/manager needs to control finances and make profitable decisions.

Section 5

Watering and Growing Care

HOW MUCH WATER?

Most plants consist primarily of water. The quality of the water they receive is extremely important. It's also very important that water samples be tested regularly during the year.

The rule of thumb for watering is to feel down into the pot a couple of inches; this soil should always be moist. Try to water enough so the soil is drenched throughout the pot. The best time to water is early morning. If the plants become dry they will stop growing, and prolonged dryness may cause stunting.

About every 10 days add a water-soluble fertilizer.

Adding more peat moss to the soil mixture will create a better water-holding capacity and more constant moisture level. Also, there are products on the market like Terra-Sorb® you can add to soil. Terra-Sorb is a synthetic copolymer capable of absorbing 300 to 400 times its weight in water. It increases the water-holding capacity of any soil mix, keeping the root zone moist but not wet. As Terra-Sorb comes in contact with water, each individual particle swells to form an insoluble gel-like nugget. The nuggets act as water reservoirs to nurture the plant. Therefore, with stress minimized, Terra-Sorb promotes strong, healthy root systems, encourages vigorous plant growth, improves survival, and results in at least a 50% reduction in water requirements. This is especially useful when potting plants or trees in larger pots. Also, when setting plants into a landscape, this product helps reduce stress from changing moisture levels. Less frequent fertilizing is necessary when using these water-holding crystals.

Plants may go for a week or so between watering during dark, cloudy weather.

Tables can be made easily and inexpensively using commercial pallets or flats. They usually come in a 4'x 4' size, perfect for this use. The benches should be arranged so watering can be done easily and quickly.

The essential conditions for rooting cuttings are moisture, air, and a certain degree of warmth. The need for moisture is obvious, since the cuttings have been isolated from their former source of supply and are in real danger of being desiccated. This applies particularly to leafy cuttings, since their leaves are still giving off or transpiring moisture. Therefore, early insertion in a medium such as moist soil, sand, or compost is essential. This is usually achieved by keeping the cuttings in a greenhouse and maintaining a humid atmosphere or by misting.

PROPAGATION

Getting plants off to the right start is the first step for any successful grower. If growing from seed, once germinated the seedling needs transplanting, whether into a soil container, the ground, or rockwool. This initial stage of propagation has different demands and requirements for temperature and moisture. If you are growing cuttings, you must allow them to have a friendly environment which encourages rooting.

Purchasing or taking cuttings from existing plants is often the preferred method of propagation. Many plants do well from cuttings, including cucumbers, tomatoes, pothos, all vines, shrubbery, foliage plants, flowers, and herbs. Rooting hormone powder on cuts is suggested. Also, use an anti-transpirant spray to eliminate the need for a high humidity area for rooting cuttings (Wilt-Pruf® is suggested).

Many books can be found on propagating plants. To avoid confusion seek out the ones that discuss your choice of crop. See pages 124-126 for a partial list.

MISTING

The rooting of softwood leafy cuttings under spray or mist is a technique now widely used by nurserymen and some beginners. The aim of misting is to continuously maintain a film of water on the leaves, thus reducing transpiration and keeping the cutting strong until rooting can take place. Cuttings can then be fully exposed to light and air without harm, because humidity remains high, preventing damage even in bright sunshine.

Misting accelerates rooting and promotes hard-to-root varieties. It will also prevent disease in cuttings by washing all fungus spores off before they can attack the tissues. While the leaves in this process must be kept continuously moist, it is important that a minimum of water is used. Excessive water leaches out nutrients from the compost and can cause starvation. Moreover, a directly injurious effect on the cutting can occur from overwatering, so it is essential to use nozzles capable of producing a very fine mist.

TIMERS

There are two methods of spray control that work very well. One uses an electric timeclock mechanism. The timeclock may be set to give a spray burst every three, five, or seven minutes. The disadvantage of this method is that the interval between misting periods remains the same regardless of weather conditions. If the timeclock is set to give a spray burst every five minutes, this might be excessive under dark weather conditions and inadequate during bright, sunny conditions.

ELECTRONIC LEAF

The second method of spray control uses a sensing element called an electronic leaf. This is used in conjunction with a solenoid valve and a switching controller installed in the water lines. The artificial leaf is placed among the cuttings and dries out or loses superficial water at exactly the same rate the cuttings do. At a certain stage of dryness the sensing element activates and opens the solenoid valve so that water is supplied to the nozzles. When moistened by the spray the electronic leaf causes the solenoid valve to close again, and misting is temporarily suspended.

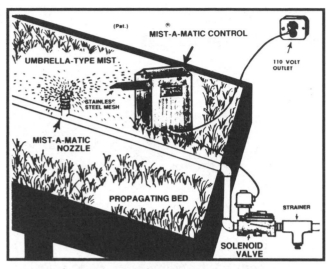

Electronic Leaf Spray Control System

This method controls the frequency of spraying periods based on temperature and light intensity. Thus, on a bright day misting might occur every 2 to 3 minutes, while on a dark day it might be at 15-minute intervals, and at night every 3 or 4 hours. Mist irrigation units can consist of one or more nozzles. Spacing of nozzles is usually 3 to 5 feet apart and 24" above the table.

OTHER TIPS

A lot of problems with greenhouse plants begin with improper watering. Too much water will cause root rot, unbalanced pH, and excess humidity. This will make the plants weak and susceptible to bugs and disease. Water must be applied before the soil is completely dry, but not while it is still quite wet. Apply water in large enough amounts to "wash" the soil in the pot. In other words, water your plants until water flows out of the holes. This is important— excess salts and fertilizers must be flushed out through the holes. Always allow soil to dry almost completely before repeating.

Watering is generally not necessary on days when clouds or rain block the sun's drying effects. Cloudy days are a good time to spray for insects and use liquid fertilizers.

Watering is best done in the morning hours on sunny days, so the plants will have time to dry before the sun gets too hot. If not, leaf damage may occur on some sensitive plants. Watering late in the afternoon is not suggested, since wet leaves at night promote fungus.

A water breaker on the end of a hose is recommended for 4" to 8" pots. This will allow you to add more water to the pots on the edges of the tables; these pots may dry out more quickly than those in the center of the tables.

DRIP IRRIGATION

Installing a drip irrigation system can be one of the most rewarding things you can do for your greenhouse crops. Not only will it save you hours on watering your plants, it will also allow your plants to grow faster and healthier, and vegetable plants will have bigger yields. Aside from adequate light, insufficient or improperly delivered water can be the biggest limiting factor in the greenhouse. A regular, consistent watering cycle is one of the secrets to getting as much as 100% more yield on vegetables, and up to twice as fast a rate of growth on most plants.

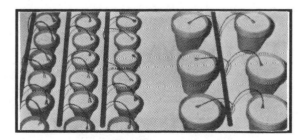

Drip Irrigation System

Designing your drip irrigation system can be as simple as using ½" to 1" poly pipe with holes punched in where small tubing is, then push. Emitters that regulate flow are then put on the other end and placed at the base of plants. Filters and pressure regulators are also needed, and are easily installed using the directions supplied with these components.

Most nursery supply businesses will help you design the best layout for your plants. This can include a fertilizer injection system to automatically feed greenhouse crops.

POT DRAINAGE

Try to let plants dry out on rainy days. Watering may cause excess salt build-up in the soil if the air temperature is too wet to let the plants dry out.

Watering during the hot months can be decreased by adding a water-absorbent material to the soil. Peat moss and vermiculite are the most popular. These soil conditioners hold up to twenty times their weight in water.

If your soil is holding too much water and you are not getting proper plant growth, it might be that you need to add more drainage material. This could be sand, pine bark, perlite, styrofoam beads, rice hulls, and peanut shells, to name a few. Pine bark and hulls add nutrition to the soil when they decay.

Make sure when purchasing a hose for watering to get the best quality rubber you can find. A cheap hose won't last long in constant use.

Sprayer heads come in many styles. We use the fan type for all spraying, a small breaker type for general watering, and a large breaker on a bend extension for hanging baskets and hard-to-reach areas.

pH: THE MOST IMPORTANT NUMBER

Although pH is not a nutrient, it can cause nutritional problems. If it's too high, the plants don't get the full value of nutrients; if it's too low, the plants get more of certain nutrients than they need, producing toxic reactions.

Low pH

At low pH readings (5.3 to 5.7), magnesium is less available and iron is more available to plants—hence the magnesium deficiency and iron toxicity reactions. To solve this, raise the pH to 6.0 and let nature make the adjustment.

High pH

Adding too much lime or using water with a high pH can cause high pH problems. pH is not the primary problem but is an agent for nutritional imbalances such as iron or possibly manganese deficiency.

Symptoms include yellowing upper foliage with new growth appearing white in severe cases. This usually occurs at pH levels above 7.0, but it can happen at levels as low as 6.7 or 6.8 if phosphorus levels are high.

How to Handle pH

Monitoring pH is a fundamental concept of horticultural production. You can produce a high quality crop if you control pH levels.

The level of pH can change rapidly, so it is important to monitor it regularly. Even with constant water pH levels, growing medium pH levels can change during a crop growth cycle.

The direction of the change depends on the material being added to the medium. If the irrigation water is high in calcium and magnesium, the pH of the medium will increase. If an acid fertilizer is used, the pH of the medium will decrease.

Peat and perlite growing mixes present unique pH reactions. Since these mixes consist primarily of peat moss, which has a low pH, growers add lime to increase the pH level. The peat must be moistened to activate the lime and raise the pH.

The problem is that this process can take up to two weeks. With crops where pH is critical to germination, growers must be aware of this time factor and premoisten the growing medium so it reaches a pH of 6.0 to 7.0 before the seeds are sown. The way to keep pH between 6.0 and 7.0 is to adjust the pH levels of both the water and fertilizer all the time. This way, additions of water or fertilizer will not change the existing medium pH. This is the safest way to ensure consistent pH readings in the recommended range.

Most growers adjust water pH by adding acids. The most popular acids are phosphoric, nitric, and sulfuric. There are also disadvantages to each of these, since not only do they lower pH but they also add nitrogen. When you add sulfuric acid, you also add sulfates.

In order to select one of these acids and determine what proportion is needed to bring your water between 6.0 and 7.0, send a water and soil sample to a soil testing laboratory. The recommended acid ratio can vary from one to four ounces per 100 gallons of water. Be sure to check the testing lab before using this method of pH control.

When you monitor and adjust pH to keep it between 6.0 and 7.0 (for foliage plants), you can change it to produce healthier, higher quality crops.

Usually when purchasing an artificial soil mixture the pH condition will be stated on the bag. This may range from 6.0 to 8.0. Try to purchase soil material with a pH close to the same as the majority of plants you will be growing without using any additives.

If the soil in pots is allowed to dry out completely a slight pH change will occur. This is not recommended. Once the soil dries out and shrinks away from the side of the pot, proper watering is hard to accomplish. In this case you must water two or three times in one hour to expand the soil again to the sides of the pot. This will allow the water to wash through the soil instead of around it.

Certain plants will definitely grow better with a high acid content in the soil. These plants include tomatoes, peppers, strawberries, and some flowers. With a high acid content they will produce much more and be far less susceptible to bugs and disease.

Most plants need a pH value of about 6.0 to 7.0. Check any good plant encyclopedia or the guide that comes with your pH meter to determine the proper pH value of a particular plant.

Some common plant diseases thrive in acid soil and are reduced by the alkalizing action of limestone. The microorganisms that produce soil antibiotics must have magnesium and calcium to kill or render harmless the microbes causing disease such as wilts, rots, or scabs. Liming acid soil mixture supplies these nutrients and increases the antibiotic-producing microbes.

WATER QUALITY

Water quality is one of the most important subjects in greenhouse production. Research done at Ohio State University by Dr. John Peterson has shown that water analysis is the most important function a grower can perform. Also, this research has disproved the belief that pH is the most important element to study when examining water. A sample's alkalinity, not its pH, is the best way to measure the influence the water will have upon the growing medium and nutrient availability.

A thorough understanding of this and how to deal with the effects of varying water quality can have an huge effect on the success of your crop. This is especially true for crops grown in soilless mediums.

TESTING PROCEDURES

Have your water tested at least twice a year; more often if possible. These evaluations should be performed by a good laboratory. You can find such laboratories listed in the yellow pages of your phone book and in Section 11 of this book. Samples should be sent in a clean, unbreakable bottle with a tight-fitting lid. Send at least one pint with very little air left on top.

Get a total water analysis done. This will cost about $15, which is relatively inexpensive compared to the impact it can have.

Your local agriculture agent can usually do a salt test for you, and it is usually free.

WHAT TO LOOK FOR

Your water analysis will show the concentration amounts of aluminum, ammonium nitrogen, nitrate nitrogen, boron, copper, chlorides, calcium, magnesium, manganese, iron, phosphorus, potassium, sodium, molybdenum, and fluorides expressed in parts per million.

Guidelines to follow for the type of plants you are growing can be found from your local extension office. Watch for excesses in calcium, magnesium, boron, sodium, chlorides, fluorides, alkalinity, and soluble salts. Extension offices are listed by state on pages 122 and 123.

WATER SUPPLY ATTENTION

When installing your main water line be sure to make it large enough to ensure proper water pressure. Usually a 1½" PVC will be large enough. Be sure to also install a valve at the entrance of the greenhouse to cut water off in case of a pipe breakage.

When installing a drip system, come off the main supply in the middle of the greenhouse to keep the pressure even at both ends. You will need a pressure valve, timer, solenoid, and a 1" poly pipe that will hold the smaller tubes that go to each plant. Complete set-up instructions are usually supplied with the tubing. Weighted emitters are put on the end of the little tube to hold the water supply in the pot or hanging basket.

WEED CONTROL

The easiest way to control weeds is through prevention. Protect soil supply from winds that carry seeds, and keep shade cloth around sides and other openings to prevent seeds from blowing in. Pull weeds before they get 3" high. To rid larger ones around greenhouses, use a general weed and grass killer like Round Up®. This is my favorite since it destroys the complete weed by imbalancing the growth pattern and is fairly safe.

Section 6
Insect and Disease Control

Keeping insects from getting out of hand is relatively easy. Trying to clean up an area after it is infested can be a lot of trouble and work. Aphids, leaf minor, and leaf-chewing worms will be your major concern. These can be kept away by spraying your foliage crop weekly. Thuricide will stop the worms. An oil base spray like Isotox will protect plants from leaf minor and a lot of the other pests that might be in your area.

An organic spray for plants infested with insects can be made using grated soap. Grate about one cup of lye soap for each one gallon of water. Spray and soak both sides of the leaf. Repeat as needed, as often as every other day.

Dipel and Thuricide are nonchemical, nonpollutant organic insecticides—two of the best for worms that chew leaves. They are relatively inexpensive and won't kill any beneficial insects (ladybugs, praying mantis, chameleons, etc.). They are both mixed with water before using.

Tobacco dust is very poisonous to most insects and can also be used on organically grown vegetables.

Diatomaceous Earth, a dust made from the grinding of a particular shell, is very good for leaf worms and is also quite inexpensive. It can be purchased at most swimming pool supply stores as filler for pool filters. Spread the dust by throwing a handful with enough speed to create a large dust cloud over the plants. This will circle the plant thoroughly with a fine dust. When soft-bodied insects get it on them, they die of dehydration. The sharp edges of the dust puncture their bodies and leave no survivors. It is advisable to wear a breathing mask when using any type of dust.

Thuricide is the liquid form of Bacillus Thurigiensis, and Dipel is the powdered dry form. When using a spraying device such as the inexpensive hozon®, which has no agitation, the liquid form stays mixed better. Dipel is used with spraying equipment that will be constantly mixing itself, such as a motor power unit. Thuricide or Dipel will not hurt animals or fish that might come in contact with water runoff. It may also be used on vegetables and herbs without any danger at all, and without any residue that could change the taste. Thuricide or Dipel should be sprayed twice, four or five days apart, in order to kill any offspring that might appear.

Safer® insecticides are my favorite. These are made with soap and pyrethrum and are completely harmless to animals and people. They can be used on just about all plants with no danger of burning the plant.

Try to spray all insecticides, fungicides, fertilizers, and growth retardants during cool morning hours. This will prevent sunburn that is quite common with some sprays. Late afternoon spraying can lead to fungus growth if plants don't dry out before dark.

Inspect your plants at the same time each day to ensure a regular growth pattern. Look for insect damage around the edges of leaves and at the center of the plant. Look for tiny eggs and scale on both sides. This is also a common place for worms to start eating. Inspect plants for fungus daily also. You will minimize losses this way. If fungus is discovered, call your local county experimental agricultural station for precise information. There are many types of fungi, and the agriculture station will be happy to help you identify your problem. Use this as a preventive procedure regularly.

Be sure to keep all dead leaves and trash off potted plants: they could start fungus. Make notes and take pictures of things you want to remember. It is a good idea to keep a log of your operation. This will give you new ideas and provide you with accurate research data later on.

DISEASES—PLANT AND SOIL

Most diseases can be avoided with proper fertilizer, soil moisture, and air circulation. Also, emphasize sanitation, eradication of diseased plants, and use of disease-resistant varieties. Sterilized soil is a great contributor to a disease-free crop. If you discover symptoms of disease contact your local agricultural experiment station to see which spray or soil drench is best for your plant type and area. Also, check your local library for an encyclopedia on plant diseases. Plant diseases can be fast or slow in showing symptoms. So at the first sign of a problem—leaf drop, spots, yellowing, tip burn, or wilting—check it and treat it as soon as possible.

ORNAMENTAL FOLIAGE PLANT DISEASES

An excellent reference book on ornamental foliage plant diseases, written by O.R. Chase, University of Florida, Central Florida Research and Education Center, is offered by the Florida Foliage Association. The 92-page *Compendium of Ornamental Foliage Plant Diseases* provides the most current, complete information on the subject for $17 postpaid. Contact FFA, P.O. Box Y, Apopka, Florida 32704.

They also have a plant locator for Florida foliage for $3. Both books are well worth the money.

FUNGI

Fungi are tiny plants that take their energy from organic matter. They do not have the ability to turn the sun's energy into food because of the lack of chlorophyll. If a fungus feeds on live matter, it is classified as a parasite; if matter is not alive, the fungus is saprophytic. The first kind will cause you trouble in the greenhouse or garden; the latter is beneficial, helping to break down organic material in the compost pile.

Fungi that affect plants are named for their appearance. Leaf spot fungi causes round, yellow or yellow-green spots that may get darker with age. Soil-inhabiting fungi cause damping off, a common disease of seedlings, and various root rots.

Safer®'s fungicide is an all-natural spray for use on vegetables, ornamentals, fruit, and flowering plants. This is an excellent spray that controls black-spot, powdery mildew, leaf spot, and rust.

If ants are a problem, boric acid is the answer. It is an old-fashioned ant killer that's more effective and economical than most chemical sprays.

ALL-NATURAL SOLUTIONS FOR GREENHOUSE PESTS

I strongly discourage using any pest control which can harm plants, people, pets, or the environment. Prevention of pests is the best cure, and this is done through maintaining a healthy crop and balanced environment. But even the most healthy greenhouse can be attacked by crop-threatening insects. The first step is to identify the insect and select the appropriate remedy. Second, choose between beneficial insects or organic pesticides, or both. Third, continue with a regular program of spraying or releasing bugs.

Learn as much about biocontrols as you can. An Extension Agent can help you set up a release program based on the pest you have and let you know of local users in the area to visit. Locate and contact suppliers well ahead of time, plan which delivery service to use, and have insulated coolers ready for storing large shipments until they can be released.

Develop good monitoring techniques such as using sticky cards, regular scouting for pests and disease, and using attracting plants.

Sticky cards—yellow for white flies, blue for thrips—are hung over crops in your greenhouse. Record the pests caught weekly (type and number) for tracking the biocontrol's progress. Scout around and make visual counts of non-mobile stages (eggs and larvae) of both pests and beneficial insects, and record type and number.

Grow a few attraction plants like ruta graveolens, or common rue. This herb is easily grown from seed and is highly attractive to white flies. Use rue to draw white flies from cash crops, reducing the amount of encarsia formosa (a parasite wasp) needed. The rue is also used as the banker plant for encarsia propagation, as well as a monitor plant. If white flies are in the green-

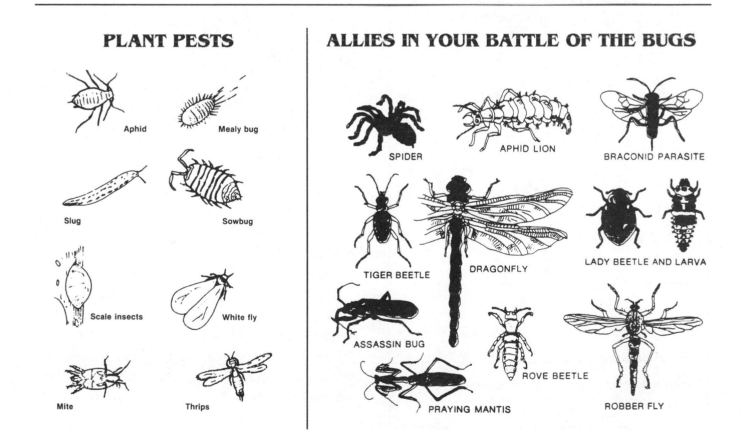

PLANT PESTS

Aphid

Mealy bug

Slug

Sowbug

Scale insects

White fly

Mite

Thrips

ALLIES IN YOUR BATTLE OF THE BUGS

SPIDER

APHID LION

BRACONID PARASITE

TIGER BEETLE

DRAGONFLY

LADY BEETLE AND LARVA

ASSASSIN BUG

ROVE BEETLE

PRAYING MANTIS

ROBBER FLY

house you'll find them on the rue plant first!

Other host plants for beneficial insects include nasturtiums, zinnias, marigolds, fennel, dill, parsley, tansy, and daisies. Grow a few to attract and feed beneficials.

Plant-derived controls—rotenone, pyrethrym, and sabadilla dust (derived from a South American plant)—leave no harmful residue to food crops and degrade quickly. Follow directions on labels carefully. Remember, these will kill beneficial insects.

Most insects will hatch faster in hotter temperatures. Be sure to consider this when scheduling spraying or beneficial insect releases.

To control insect pests, it is important to know something about their life cycles and feeding habits. By monitoring your sticky traps and consulting your Extension Agent you will soon be an expert.

BENEFICIAL INSECTS

	approx. release amounts
Predator Mites	1-10 per plant
Persimilis	1-10 per plant
(55-80°F, 70-90% humidity)	
Californicus	1-10 per plant
(60-100°+, 60-90% humidity)	
Ladybugs *(seasonal)*	1,000 per 3,000 sq. ft.
Aphid Predators	1-2 midge cocoons per plant
Whitefly Parasites	1 per sq. ft. x 4 applications
Trichogramma Wasps	1 card per greenhouse (thousands of eggs)
Green Lacewing Eggs	1000 eggs per 900 sq. ft.
Mealybug Predators	2-5 per plant
Beneficial Nematodes	1 mil per 3,000 sq. ft.
Scale Predators	2-5 per plant
Praying Mantis Egg Case	200 mantis per egg case 3 cases per greenhouse

Beneficial Insects — Types and Requirements

WASP – My favorites are braconid wasps for tomato horn worms; chalcid wasps for aphids, scales, mealy bugs, and moths; and encarsia formosa for white flies.

BENEFICIAL NEMATODES – Any insect that spends time in the ground is vulnerable to attack by these tiny insect parasites, such as beetles, cutworms, wireworms, bores, and root maggots. Application is easy: just spray solution onto soil surface that contains nematodes.

LADYBUGS - Usually used along with other beneficial insects to achieve maximum results. Their diet includes aphids, scale, mites, mealy bugs, white flies, and eggs of many other insects.

GREEN LACEWINGS – These delicate-looking insects can munch out on a wide range of greenhouse pests including aphids, spider mites, thrips, mealy bugs, white flies, and immature scales.

PRAYING MANTIS – My favorite to watch at work! They have a wide-ranging insect diet including aphids, beetles, caterpillars, moths, grasshoppers, and mosquitoes. Egg clusters contain 200–300 eggs. Use with other biocontrols.

PREDATORY MITES – The loracious predatory mite phytoseiulus persimills is the all-around favorite for red and two-spotted spider mites when temperatures are below 85°F. Use Californicus when temperatures are over 90°F. Be patient and give them time to work.

CHAMELEONS – In warm climates these lizards do a fine job patrolling crops like stock spider plants, where the only pests of much concern are tomato hornworms and cabbage loopers. Growers in the South can collect these around ponds and rivers with butterfly nets. A real pleasure while growing plants is seeing these beautiful lime green creatures watch over their staked-out territory and communicate with other lizards using body motions.

MOST COMMON INSECTS

Mealy Bugs and Scale Insects

Sooner or later you will come across scale insects or mealy bugs with their cotton-like look. They prefer cacti, fig varieties, palms, and succulents; they also attack many others.

It is important to take care of this problem immediately. Treat for mealy bugs and scale insects the same way: spray three times at intervals of 8 days.

Mealy bugs spin a waxy cover for protection. They look like small dots of cotton.

Scale insects move only in larvae stage (time to spray), then grow a strong shield that can protect them from insecticides and other threats. Under the shield they will produce several hundred eggs which hatch and spread over the plant. Some shields may stay in place after the scale has died. To begin spraying, you must wait until larvae begins to spread.

White Fly

These two-millimeter-long white insects flutter into the air when the host plant is under attack. Eggs will be found on the underside of young leaves. They will appear as white patches and will hatch in 8 to 15 days. The larvae will then spend their time eating the undersides of the leaves.

Its favorite flowers are geraniums, poinsettias, and impatiens. Its favorite vegetables are tomatoes, peppers, and cucumbers.

Leaf Minor

Adult leaf minor are small black flies that deposit eggs under the leaf epidermis. When hatched, the larvae eat between the upper and lower leaf epidermis, consuming the soft tissue that is found between veins.

Their scarring tunnels are serpentine or blotchy looking and become brownish-tan as tissue dies. This damage is the early warning of the presence of this insect.

Systemic insecticide, which is put on the soil surface and absorbed by the plant, is the best way to rid plants of this invader. Regular spraying of crops with a soap or pyrethrin base spray can prevent attack.

Aphids

Aphids are the most common and widespread of all pests found in the greenhouse. They live in colonies and attack young shoot tips and flower buds.

These insects are rather small. Their size ranges from 1/16" to 1/8" long. They are oval-shaped and move very slowly.

The aphid is a fast breeder, giving birth to live young in the summer when the weather is warm. They lay eggs in the late summer for fall.

This next generation can in turn give birth in seven days to another generation, and so on. You can see how simple it is to become infested with aphids if close inspection is neglected.

Their main food is the sap they suck in large quantities from the veins of the plant.

Spider Mites

Spider mites are identified by their fine network of webs on the underside of leaves. Good plant hygiene and proper growing conditions are the best prevention for attack.

The spider mites are very small, only ½ to 1 millimeter long. To examine for them properly, you need a magnifying glass. This is why it is so important to look closely when inspecting plants.

Biological warfare is most effective for professional tomato and cucumber growers. The predatory mite is used to eat up spider mites, and is widely available today. Check with large seed companies to order these.

USE OF NATURAL SOLUTIONS ON GREENHOUSE PLANTS

INSECT	CONTROL SPRAYS, DUSTS, & BENEFICIAL INSECTS
red & two-spotted spider mites	Safer® insecticidal soap; predatory mites–phytoseiulus persimilis (55°–80°F air temp); californicus (90°–100°F+). *Remarks:* Very small pest. Can be seen with hand lens. Mites have sucking mouth parts and cause yellowish spots on leaves. Leaf drop is common. Check plants often for mites. They are more numerous during hot, dry weather. Use 2 spray applications, 5 to 7 days apart. Release predatory mites as soon as spider mites are found, one per plant, plus one more for every infested leaf. Continue weekly until at least one predator is on each infested leaf.
scale & mealy bugs	Safer® soap; cryptolaemus montrouzieri chalcid wasp, ladybugs, green lacewings. *Remarks:* Repeat applications until all pests are killed. Wasps and lacewings need pollen-bearing plants for food.
aphids	Safer®; aphidoletes aphidimyza (aphid midge); aphidius matricariae (wasp); chrysopa spp (lacewings). *Remarks:* Aphids attack young tender growth, causing leaf curl and sooty mold. Check new growth for reinfestation. Release aphid midge cocoons at a rate of 3 to 5 per sq. yard, weekly, until control is noticed (usually 2 to 4 applications).
white flies	Safer®; encarsia formosa (tiny wasp), delphastus pusillus (black lady beetle). *Remarks:* Underside of leaves must be sprayed every 5 to 7 days in moderate temperatures; every 3 days in hot weather. White flies cause black sooty mold. Encarsia is released weekly one pupa per four plants, 8 to 10 weeks on tomato crops.
thrips	Amblyseius cucumeris, a. barkeri (predatory mites), syrphid flies, lacewings. *Remarks:* Check plants often for this very small sucking insect that discolors plant foliage. Success with these predators depends on releasing them as soon as (or before) the first thrips are detected.
hornworms, caterpillars, cabbage loopers, cutworms	Bacillus Th (Dipel, Thuricide, Biotrol), tachinid flies; trichogramma, braconid, and ichneumon (wasp). *Remarks:* Tiny wasp that lays eggs in worms, caterpillars. Harmless to people and pets.
leaf minors	Pyrethin; dacnusa sibirica, diglyphus isaca. *Remarks:* Dispose of heavily infested plants. Spray at 4-day intervals.

Be sure to follow the dealer's recommendations.

RECOMMENDED RATES FOR USE OF INSECTICIDES AND FUNGICIDES
(read product label for details)

INSECTICIDES	LEVEL TEASPOONS PER GAL.	QTY. PER 100 GALLONS	APHIDS	ARMYWORMS	BAGWORMS	BEETLES	BIRCH LEAF MINER	BLACK VINE WEEVIL	CABBAGE LOOPER	CANKERWORM	CATERPILLAR	CUTWORM	CYCLAMEN MITE	FUNGUS GNATS	GYPSY MOTHS	LACE BUGS	LEAFHOPPER	LEAFMINER	LEAFROLLER	MEALY BUGS	MITES	NEMATODES	SCALE	SLUGS-SNAILS	THRIP	WEBWORM	WHITE FLIES	GENERAL PURPOSE	VEGETABLES
Ambush*	SEE LABEL																	■											•
Avid		8 oz.																■			•								
Biovector	SEE LABEL													•															
Citation	SEE LABEL																	■											
Cygon 2E	1-4	1-4 Pts.	•																										
Decathlon	1/5	21 Tsp.	•	•	•				•		•			•	•	•	•		•	•	•		•		•	•	•	■	
Dibrom	Vaporize	1 Oz./10,000 Cu. Ft.	•																•							•		•
Dipel BT	1/2-4	1/4-2 Lb.							■		■				■														•
Dipel 4L	1/2-4	1/2-4 Pts.									■				■														•
Discus	SEE LABEL						■																						
Dursban 2EC	1-2	1-2 Pts.	•		•						•							•		•	•					•	•	•	
Dursban 50WP		1/2-1 Lb.	•		•						•							•		•	•					•	•	•	
Dycarb	2-8	10-40 Oz.	■					■												•			•					•	
Empire 20	1-2	1-2 Pts.	•		•						•							•		•	•					•	•	•	
Enstar	1/2-1-1/4	8-20 Oz.	•											•						■			•				•		
Gnatrol	2-8	2-8 Pts.												■															
Grandslam		1-4 Lbs.	•																	•				■					
Guthion 50% WP*	2-4	1-2 Lb.	•													•	•			•			•		•				•
Imidan 50WP	2-1/2 to 3-1/2	1 to 1-1/2 Lb.					•			•					•														•
Isotox Spray	1-2	1-2 Pts.																										•	
Joust	1/4-1/2	4-8 Oz.																		■							■		
Kelthane 35	3 to 4-1/2	1 to 1-1/2 Lb.											•								•								•
Knox Out 2FM	1/2-1 Oz.	3-6 Pts.	•											•			•	•		•	•		•		•			•	
Lannate L*	1-2	1-2 Pts.							■		■								•		•								
Lannate 90% WP*	1/2-1	1/4 to 1/2 Lb.		•					■		■								•		•								
Mavrik		2-5 Oz.	■								•									•	■						•	■	
Meta-Systox R	1-2	1-2 Pts.	•															•			•								
Monitor L*	1/2-2	1/2-2 Lb.	•									•					•				•						•		•
Orthene 75%	3/4 to 1-1/2	1/3-2/3 Lb.	•								•					■			•		•						•		
Oxamyl 10G	1.4-1.9 Lbs Per 1000 Sq. Ft.		•			•		•			•						•	•		•	•	•	•				•	•	
Pentac Aqua Flow	1/2	1/2 Pt.																			•								
Pentac WP	2	8 Oz.																			■								
PT 1200														•													•	•	
PT 1300			•						•	•	•				•	•	•	•	•	•			•				•	•	
PT 1700			•																	•					•		•	•	
Safer Soap	9-18		•								•			•		•	•			•	•		•				•		•
Scalecide	15-24	2-3 Gal.																					■						
Sevimol	3	1 Lb.																										•	•
Sumithrin	1-2	1-2 Pts.	•															•		•							■		
Sunspray	SEE LABEL		•			•					•			•		•	•			•	•		■				•		■
Talstar		6-32 Oz.	■																		•						■	■	
Tame	1/3-1	5.3-16 Oz.	•	•		•											•	•	•		•						■		
Thiodan 50% WP	3	1 Lb.																			•								
Vendex 50WP		1/2-1 Lb.	•																		•								•
Victory	1/2-4	1/2-4 Pts.							■	■					■														■
Vydate L*	2-4	2-4 Pt.																			•	■					•	■	•
X-Clude																											•	

LEGEND — ■: THE ITEMS MARKED ■ ARE LABELLED FOR THIS SPECIFIC INSECT, AND ARE THE INSECTICIDES MOST WIDELY USED. • THE ITEMS MARKED • ARE LABELLED FOR THE INSECT CONTROL INDICATED. *: APPLICATORS PERMIT REQUIRED.

NO RECOMMENDATIONS EXPRESS OR IMPLIED ARE MADE BY PUBLISHER FOR THESE PRODUCTS.

Section 7
Soil and Fertilizer Mixtures

PLANT NUTRITION AND GROWING MEDIUMS

Production of high quality potted crops depends on an optimum growing environment. Good growing practices will enhance plant quality, beginning with the selection of a good growing medium. Several growing mediums can be used interchangeably for different crops, but production systems such as propagation may favor one type of medium over another.

It is not always possible to make generalizations about the watering needs of a medium. The crop and greenhouse environment will influence the frequency of application. Growing mediums composed of coarse ingredients require more frequent watering than those made with smaller components. The grower must adjust his watering practices accordingly.

Plant nutrition and growing mediums go hand in hand, since plants normally obtain most of their fertilizer nutrients via root uptake from the growing medium. As nutrient levels in a medium decrease due to root uptake or leaching, plant quality may decline if the level falls below the required minimum. This is more likely when fertilizer is applied infrequently or is followed by successive applications of plain water. To maintain required nutrient levels, water-soluble fertilizer should be applied with each application of water (constant liquid feeding).

WATER-SOLUBLE FERTILIZERS

In selecting a fertilizer, it is essential to consider both the particular crop and the growing medium. Crops differ in their nutrient requirements. As for growing mediums, modern-day soilless mixes will give best results when Peat-Lite fertilizers are used. A dominant feature of the Peters® Peat-Lite formulations is a higher percentage of nitrate nitrogen compared to the ammoniacal and urea forms. Peters® Peat-Lites also contain higher levels of minor elements necessary for proper nutrition in soilless growing mediums.

Peat-Lite fertilizers can also be used if soil is a component of the medium. Use Peat-Lite formulations if the soil component is 20% or less by volume. It is good practice to have the soil analyzed separately in advance for nutrient elements, and especially for the minor elements so that excessive levels do not occur.

MINOR ELEMENTS

Fertilizers are available with a high percentage of nitrate nitrogen and a low percentage of minor elements. An example is Peters® 20-10-20 General Purpose, which is suggested for growing mediums with greater than 20% soil content or if the soil contains high minor element levels. With this formulation, plants can benefit from the high nitrates with lower additions of minor elements, as needed.

Plants will get off to a fast start if they are fertilized early. The time to start fertilizing is at planting. This is true for seedlings and rooted cuttings; they are not too tender, as was commonly believed at one time. The modern approach is to begin fertilizing right away.

Geographical areas differ in terms of water quality. For this reason, the longer term response of the plant to a fertilizer program can be affected by the inherent components of the irrigation water. For example, boron is often too high in irrigation water sources. In this situation, select a fertilizer which is low in boron or is boron-free. Water analysis will provide the fine-tuning necessary to select the optimum fertilizer for a specific growing situation.

Where soil-containing mediums have acceptable minor element levels and there is no need for elevated minors in the fertilizer, growers can choose from many fertilizers with reduced minor elements. Typical of these formulas is the most popular 20-20-20 General Purpose. Other popular formulas include 15-30-15 and 20-5-30. Formulations with reduced minor and high nitrates are 15-15-15 and 16-4-12. Since both of these may contain sodium, it is helpful to know whether the irrigation water contains a high sodium level; this could make the use of 15-15-15 or 16-4-12 inadvisable with crops other than lilies.

ARTIFICIAL SOIL

The best soil for container planting is one that allows water to pass through easily. The mixture should be pH-adjusted to grow the plant variety you want. This is one of the main keys to realizing profits from growing greenhouse plants. Jiffy Mix is a good soil substitute mixture. It is composed of shredded sphagnum peat moss, horticultural grade vermiculite, and certain other elements. Pro Mix and Metro Mix are equally good. I mostly use Metro Mix 500 with a pH of about 7.0. Perlite is another useful additive. It is completely sterile and allows good drainage. You can make your own soil substitute by combining one part vermiculite, one part perlite, and one to two parts shredded peat moss. For plants requiring a somewhat alkaline soil add pulverized limestone. Sterile soil should be used wherever possible. You can also easily sterilize soil at home using commercial soil sterilizers, or by putting it in your home oven for ten minutes at 350°.

Sometimes sand is used alone. Although it is a very good rooting medium, cuttings planted in this must be transferred into soil as soon as they have rooted, since sand has no plant nutrients. You can also get good results with a mixture of peat and sand. Suitable proportions are two parts sand and one part peat. Such a compost, while being well aerated, also retains moisture. Practically all cuttings may be rooted in this successfully.

Another good mixture is two parts sand and one part sphagnum moss. This compost is prepared by chopping up the moss very fine, being sure it is mixed well. When kept moist, this is an excellent medium for difficult cuttings. When filling 6" pots and larger, a mixture that is less expensive than a commercially prepared one might be desired. This may consist of topsoil

HYDRO SOL—PETERS 5-11-26

Guaranteed Analysis

Total Nitrogen (N)..5%
  5.00% Nitrate Nitrogen
Available Phosphoric
  Acid (P_2O_5)..11%
Soluble Potash (K_2O)....................................26%
Magnesium (Mg) 3.11%
Boron (B)..0.050%
Copper (Cu) 0.015%
Iron (Fe) 0.300%
Manganese (Mn) 0.050%
Molybdenum (Mo)...0.010%
Zinc (Zn)...0.015%

Primary Plant Nutrient Sources: Potassium Nitrate, Potassium Phosphate. Potential basicity 60 lbs. Calcium Carbonate equivalent per ton.

Designed to serve as a base foundation for hydroponic growing systems. Possesses outstanding solubility so important in hydroponic operations. Provides all major, secondary and trace elements except calcium.

USES:
- For all types of hydroponic production.
- Widely used in hydroponic vegetable production units.

DESCRIPTION	PKG.	PRICE/ BAG
Hydrophonic Tomato 5-11-26	25 lb.	$31.30

GENERAL PURPOSE—PETERS 20-20-20

Originally widest selling fertilizer, safely used on wide variety of crops. Particularly good where no fertility correction is needed. Formula is acidic, nitrogen source is largely ammonic (75%).

Guaranteed Analysis

Total Nitrogen (N)...20%
  5.61% Nitrate Nitrogen
  3.96% Ammoniacal Nitrogen
  10.43% Urea Nitrogen
Available Phosphoric
  Acid (P_2O_5)..20%
Soluble Potash (K_2O)..20%
Primary Plant Nutrient Sources: Urea, Ammonium Phosphate, Potassium Nitrate. Potential acidity 597 lbs. Calcium Carbonate equivalent per ton.

USES:
- Bedding plants, pot plants and nursery crops.
- Feeding of turf, ornamentals and shade trees.
- Good for use in high pH situations.

Net Weight 25 Pounds (11.34 kg)

20-20-20 GENERAL PURPOSE FEED

1-3 BAGS	4-39 BAGS	40-79 BAGS	80 & UP BAGS
$22.45	$21.55	$20.05	$19.10

GRACE—METRO MIX 300S

USES:
1. Outstanding growing on mix for pots and baskets

INGREDIENTS:
1. Canadian Sphagnum Peat Moss
2. No. 3 Grade Horticultural Vermiculite
3. Tested Wetting Agent
4. Starter Nutrient Charge
5. Composted Pine Bark
6. Ground Polystyrene
7. Washed Granite Sand

Package size — 3 cubic foot bag.

Average weight 13-16 lbs. per cubic foot

pH after wetting: 5.2-6.5

1-24 BGS.	25-49 BGS.	50-99 BGS.	100-UP BGS.
$9.00	$8.55	$8.10	$7.55

CROP & FORMULA APPLICATION GUIDE

CROP	15-0-15 CAL SPECIAL	17-17-17 GERANIUM & BEDDING PLANT SPECIAL	20-5-30 HI-NITRATE SPECIAL	20-10-20 GENERAL PURPOSE LOW PHOSPHATE	20-20-20 GENERAL PURPOSE	28-18-8 HI-ACID	10-20-30 POTASH SPECIAL	12-31-14 PURPOSE HIGH PHOSPHATE
African Violets							●	
Annual & Bedding Plants		●	▲	▲			X	
Azaleas				△	●			
Boston Fern							●	
Begonias — Tuberous	▲	●						
Blooming Pot Plants							●	
Blueberries					●			
Camellias				●				
Carnations				△				
Cacti & Succulents	▲	●						
Chrysanthemums	▲		△			▲		
Cinerarias		●						
Cuttings							●	
Cyclamen								
Ferns				●			▲	
Field Transplants							∧	
Foliage Plants			△	●				
Gardenias				●				
Geraniums	▲	●	△				X	
Gerbera	▲		●				X	
Gloxinias		△	●				X	
Hydrangeas				●			△	
Kalanchoe			●					
Lilies	●	△	△				X	
Nursery Stock				△				
Orchids								
Pink Hydrangeas							X	
Poinsettias			△				X	
Pansies	▲	●						
Pot Mums			●				X	
Roses		△						
Rhododendrons					●		▲	
Seedlings								
Snapdragons				△			●	
Transplants (All)							●	
Tropical Foliage			●	△	△			
Tomatoes							●	
Vegetables				●			X	
Woody Ornaments				●				

SYMBOLS:

X Starter. Switch to special formulation after root mass is well developed.

● Appropriate crop formula.

△ Alternate to appropriate formula.

▲ Use as a crop toner or for a ready source of calcium and magnesium.

mixed with drainage material such as pine shavings, sand, rice or peanut hulls, peat moss, sawdust, perlite, styrofoam, vermiculite, or humus.

I find that a rich humas type topsoil mixed with pine shavings at a two to one ratio (two parts soil, one part shavings) to be very good. Humus or peat moss are excellent soil additives. They soak up moisture during watering and then meter it out slowly while it dries out.

VERMICULITE

Vermiculite is exploded mica. The layers of mica separate when heated and each layer can then hold a film of water. It will not pack down and therefore holds air between the pieces of mica. Air around the roots is necessary to prevent them from drowning.

Use large vermiculite for soil mixing and the small, fine type for starting seeds.

PERLITE

Perlite looks like coarse white sand, only larger. It is formed when obsidian, a glassy volcanic rock, is heated. Like vermiculite, it holds large amounts of water and doesn't pack down, leaving plenty of air in the soil.

There are no minerals available from vermiculite or perlite, and just a few from peat moss.

pH BALANCE

All plants grow differently. Some grow fast and tall, some short and slow. They require different soil and amounts of water. The pH amount states the acid or alkaline amount in the soil. Anything wet, or capable of being dissolved in water, has some potential for absorbing and retaining the element of hydrogen. The greater the potential for absorbing and retaining, the more alkaline it becomes.

The pH scale describes the amount of hydrogen a substance can hold. The median of the readings is 7.0 on a scale ranging from 0 to 14. A soil test kit costing around $10 will allow you to determine the pH of your soil. It is a simple test. A pH reading of 7.0 indicates an alkaline soil; anything below 7.0 means the soil is more acid than alkaline.

Plants show signs of improper pH quickly. Growth may slow noticeably; leaves will wilt, become yellow and drop off; and the plant may lose its flowers. Peat moss, topsoil, or humus can be added to a soil mix to increase acidity. Limestone, perlite, or hydronated lime are all very alkaline substances.

When you are getting too much salt build-up in your soil it will show around the edges and at the holes of your pots. You will notice a white to yellow-white substance that looks like a crust of powder. This can be taken care of by simply washing the soil with water. Give each pot about one inch of water twice a day for two days; then let the pots dry out slightly. A more severe problem may require that this process be repeated.

If you are using drip irrigation, leave the system on for at least 24 hours. This is also a good practice a few days before each shipment. It will rid pots of any excess salt that may harm plants during the extreme changes of climate and light conditions during shipping, and keep quality at its highest.

Be sure not to ship pots soaking wet. Let them dry out to a damp soil before shipping (approximately two to three days depending on weather conditions).

To correct a soil that is too acid, mix a small amount of limestone or hydronated lime to sweeten the soil. Your county extension office can test your soil and suggest how to correct any problem. To raise the pH value of the soil by one unit, use about ½-pound of limestone for each ten cubic feet of soil.

Foliage plants require relatively large amounts of nitrogen, potassium, and phosphorus; and lesser amounts of calcium, magnesium, iron, zinc, and several other elements.

Nitrogen helps stimulate steady plant growth. It also strengthens the plants, and is one element which is indirectly responsible for the characteristic green color of plant foliage.

Potassium helps a plant resist disease and is one of the components necessary for manufacturing plant sugars and starches. It is also important in developing strong, healthy roots.

Phosphorus is a vital part of the production of "food" within a plant. It also triggers the mechanism by which energy, released by the sugars being "burned off" within the plant, is distributed to its various parts. Phosphorus encourages strong, disease-resistant roots.

Nitrogen, potassium and phosphorus are absolutely essential for plant health and growth. Calcium, magnesium and sulfur are also important, but they are required in smaller amounts. Calcium influences the growth of plant cells and the root system. Magnesium is important for manufacturing chlorophyll, the substance that gives plants their color. Chlorophyll is, in turn, a part of the process of photosynthesis by which a plant generates further energy for growth.

Trace elements must also be present in very small amounts. Iron, zinc, manganese, boron, molybdenum, copper, and chlorine are all trace elements.

A well-balanced fertilizer like 14-14-14 or 18-6-12 Osmocote® slow release is used by a lot of plant growers. This pellet type fertilizer lasts three to twelve months depending on formulation. The fertilizer is washed into the soil every time the plant is watered, which is the best way. A liquid fertilizer can also be applied at regular intervals.

Peters® and Nutri-Leaf® are two good water-soluble brands. They contain a dark-blue dye that will show you if your fertilizer is mixed properly by the change in color while spraying.

When applying fertilizer, follow the label directions. Peters® suggests daily or weekly applications with a mild mixture rather than a stronger solution once a month.

Osmocote® can also be mixed into the pot after filling it with soil. The amount can vary from four to ten grams for a 4½" pot. The best way to judge this is to experiment with different amounts. I use six grams in each 4½" pot, and find this ideal. After measuring the correct amount with a spoon (six grams is approximately one teaspoon), the soils must be mixed thoroughly to prevent burning of young roots. Pull all weeds at the first sign. They will use fertilizer faster than your plants.

Be sure not to overfeed your plants. Leaf burn will appear as an orange, yellow, or brown patch if too much fertilizer is applied. Usually this will appear quickly—within one or two days. It will show up on all the plants treated (whereas if it were a fungus, disease, or mineral deficiency it would generally be located in one or two areas).

If a burn does occur and the plants have leaves that can be trimmed with scissors, do so. Then drench the soil heavily—about 2" of water in each pot, to wash excess fertilizer out.

OSMOCOTE: CONTROLLED-RELEASE FERTILIZER

Osmocote® is a controlled-release fertilizer composed of small granules of a water-soluble nutrient which has been coated with a fine film of plastic resin. By following the principle of osmosis, the soluble fertilizer moves through the thin resin coating and delivers to the soil a controlled amount of nutrients over a long period of time.

In effect each Osmocote granule acts as a tiny storehouse of liquid fertilizer. It will last for up to four months if thoroughly mixed in the planting mediums, and from four to six months if put only on top of the planting mediums.

Osmocote can be used as a single supply of fertilizer or combined with your regular fertilization program.

When used as directed, there isn't any danger of burning crops. For second and third crops grown in soil to which Osmocote has been applied, the recommended rates should be reduced by 25% to 50% to compensate for nutrients carried over from previous applications.

Steaming of soil will not damage the resin coating. However, it will produce moisture and activate the nutrient-releasing processes. The grower should note this and act accordingly.

Osmocote 14-14-14
3 to 4 months

The 1:1:1 ratio of N-P-K is ideal for low soil or soilless mixes. It is an excellent formula for bedding plants, foliage, and pot plant crops.

Osmocote 19-6-12
3 to 4 months

The 3:1:2 ratio of N-P-K is formulated for mixes containing some soil, and for plants that require higher levels of nitrogen.

Osmocote 13-13-13
8 to 9 months

The 1:1:1 N-P-K formula is ideal for longer-term foliage and pot plant crops. This product is similar to 14-14-14; it just lasts longer.

Osmocote 18-6-12
8 to 9 months

Designed for longer-term greenhouse and container stock, this formula is ideal for year-round feeding. It is used for propagation and fall feeding.

Osmocote 18-6-12 Fast Start
8 to 9 months

Same as 18-6-12 regular. The only difference is its fast start characteristic.

Osmocote 17-7-12
12 to 14 months

A special formula engineered for maximum long-term feeding programs—both greenhouse and container stock.

Sierrablen 18-7-10 (+Iron)
8 to 9 months

Designed for longer-term foliage and container stock. Ideal for "once a season" feeding.

A GUIDE TO NUTRIENT-DEFICIENCY SYMPTOMS

PRIMARY NUTRIENTS	DEFICIENCY SYMPTOMS
Nitrogen	Stems are thin, erect, and hard. Leaves are smaller than normal, pale green or yellow. Lower leaves are affected first, but all leaves may be deficient in severe cases. Plants grow slowly.
Phosphorus	Stems are thin and shortened. Leaves develop purple coloration, first on undersides and later throughout. Plants grow slowly and maturity is delayed.
Potassium	Older leaves develop gray or tan areas near the margins. Eventually a scorch around the entire leaf margin may occur. Chlorotic areas may develop throughout leaf.

SECONDARY & MICRO-NUTRIENTS	DEFICIENCY SYMPTOMS
Boron	Growing points (i.e., stems) are shortened and hard; leaves are distorted. Boron will cause burnt tips to spider plants. A boron-free fertilizer should be used.
Calcium	Stem elongation is restricted by death of the growing point. Root tips die and root growth is restricted.
Iron	Distinct yellow or white areas appear between the veins of the youngest leaves.
Magnesium	Initially older leaves show yellowing between the veins. Continued deficiency causes younger leaves to become affected. Older leaves may fall with prolonged deficiency.
Manganese	Yellow mottled areas (not as intense as with iron deficiency) appear on the youngest leaves. This eventually results in an overall pale appearance.
Molybdenum	Leaves are pale, distorted, and very narrow, with some interveinal yellowing on older leaves.
Zinc	Small reddish and brown spots appear on cotyledon leaves of some plants. Green and yellow broad stripes and interveinal yellowing with marginal burning.

PLANT PROBLEMS GUIDE

SYMPTOMS	POSSIBLE CAUSES	POSSIBLE CURES
Dying young plants	Fertilizer burn	Mix fertilizer thoroughly
	Damp off disease	Use fungicide
Stunted plants (pale to yellow)	Low soil fertility	Soil test for fertilizer recommendations
	Poor soil drainage	Add aerating material
	Shallow watering	Water more heavily
Stunted plants	Extreme temperatures	Raise or lower temperatures
	Low pH	Add lime
Purplish color	Lack of phosphorus	Add phosphorus fertilizer
Holes in leaves	Insects or hail	Spray or dust
Spots, molds	Disease	Use control methods
Darkened areas on leaves	Chemical burn	Use recommended chemicals at correct rate and time
	Fertilizer burn	Keep fertilizer off plants
Wilting plants	Dry soil	Water regularly
	Excess soil moisture	Avoid overwatering
	Disease	Use resistant varieties
Weak, spindly plants	Too much shade	Adjust shading
	Plants too thick	Seed at recommended rate
	Too much nitrogen	Avoid excess fertilizer

SOIL MIX CALCULATION CHART

The following charts are for reference only. Your actual yield may be more or less, depending on many factors (such as pot or flat selected and actual filling and compaction technique).

CONTAINER SIZE & TYPE	APPROX. # OF POTS WITH 1 CU. FT.
3" Standard	100-120
6" Standard	13-15
3" Square	120-140
4" Square	35-45
4½" Geranium	30-40
4" Azalea	50-60
6" Azalea	15-18
8" Azalea	6-7
8" Hanging Pot	9-11
10" Hanging Pot	5-6

CONTAINER TYPE & SIZE	APPROX. # PER CU. FT.
1020 Flat	3-4
601 Insert	3-4
606 Insert	4-5
801 Insert	3-4
806 Insert	5-6
Fiber Pak #144	18-22
Fiber Pak #2R86	6-7
1 Gal. Container	11
3 Gal. Container	3
5 Gal. Container	2

COMMON ORGANIC FERTILIZERS FOR HERBS

FERTILIZER	ANALYSIS IN PERCENT (FRESH WEIGHT)		
	Nitrogen N	Phosphorus P_2O_5	Potassium K_2O
Blood (a very rapidly available organic fertilizer)	10	1.5	0
Fish emulsion	1	1	1
Guano: bat	6	9	3
bird	13	11	3
Kelp or seaweed	1	0.5	9
Manure: cattle	0.5	0.3	0.5
chicken	0.9	0.5	0.8
horse	0.6	0.3	0.6
sheep	0.9	0.5	0.8
swine	0.6	0.5	0.4
Meals: bone, raw	4	22	0
bone, steamed	2	27	0
cocoa shell	2.5	1	3
cotton seed	6	2.5	2
oyster shells	0.2	0.3	0
Rice hulls (ground)	0.5	0.2	0.5

Section 8
Wholesale Price List

The following lists are designed to be used as guides. Prices may vary from area to area.

FOLIAGE PLANTS	4"	6"	8"	10"	14"
Aglaonema	3.00	5.00	7.00	8.00	
Aloe	1.50	2.00	4.00	5.50	
Anthurium	3.00	5.00	7.00	8.00	12.50
Aralia "Elegantissima"	1.50	2.50	4.00	5.50	17.50
Arboricola	1.50	2.50	4.00	5.50	17.50
Baby's Tears (HB)			4.50	6.50	
Cactus	1.50	2.50	4.50	6.50	
Caladium	1.50	2.50	4.00	5.50	
China Doll (HB)			4.50	6.50	
Cordatum/Philodendron (HB)			4.50	6.50	
Cordyline Terminals		2.50	4.00	5.50	17.50
Creeping Charlie (HB)			4.50	6.50	
Cotyledon	1.50	2.50	4.00	6.50	
Diffenbachia	2.50	5.00	7.00	10.00	
Dracaena Marginate	2.50	4.00	5.50	7.50	
Eucalyptus	1.50	2.50	4.00	5.50	7.50

HB - Hanging Basket

FOLIAGE PLANTS (continued)	4"	6"	8"	10"	14"
Boston Ferns (HB)			4.50	6.50	
Bird's Nest	1.50	2.50	4.00	4.00	10.00
Rabbit's Foot (HB)			4.50	7.00	
Sprengerii	.75	1.25	2.50	4.00	
Staghorn (on wood slabs)	1.50	2.50	4.00		15.00
Ficus Benjamin Bush		2.25	3.50	4.50	17.50
Variegated Bush		2.50	3.50	5.50	17.50
Standard (tree type)		2.50	4.00	5.50	17.50
Varigated Standard		2.50	4.00	8.50	25.00
Tree Braided		4.00	5.00	8.00	25.00
Ficus Elastical/Rubber Tree		2.50	4.00	5.50	17.50
Gerbera Daisy		3.00	4.50		
Jade Plant	1.50	2.50	4.00	5.50	10.00
Jerusalem Cherry	1.50	4.00	7.00	8.00	
Kalanchoe	1.50	2.50	4.00	5.00	
Living Stones	1.50	2.50	5.00	6.00	
Norfolk Island Pine	1.50	2.50	4.00	6.00	12.50
Palms: Areca	1.50	2.50	4.00	6.00	
Chamaerops	2.00	4.00	8.00	10.00	
Fishtail	2.00	4.00	7.00	8.50	
Ponytail	2.00	3.50	4.50	10.00	
Peperomia	1.50	2.50	4.00	5.50	
Polka-Dot Plant	1.50	2.50	4.00	5.50	
Schefflera	1.50	2.50	4.00	5.50	17.50
Selloum/Philodendron		2.50	4.00	5.50	17.50
Snake/Mother-in-Law Tongs		2.00	3.00	4.00	
Spathiphyllum	2.00	3.50	4.50	6.50	17.50
Spider Plant (HB)	1.50	2.50	4.50	6.50	
String-of-Beads	1.50	2.50	4.50	6.50	
Swedish Ivy	1.50	2.50	4.50	6.50	

HB - Hanging Basket

FOLIAGE PLANTS (continued)	4"	6"	8"	10"	14"
Taro/Elephant Ears		3.00	4.50	7.50	10.00
Wandering Jew	1.50	2.00	3.00	4.00	
Yucca Cane (3 plants/pot)	2.00	3.50	4.50	6.50	17.50
Zebra Plant	1.50	2.50	4.50	5.50	

FLOWERING PLANTS	4"	6"	10"
Achimenes	1.50	2.25	3.50
African Violets	2.00	3.50	6.00
Amaryllis	2.00	3.50	6.00
Annuals	1.00	2.00	3.50
Azaleas	1.50	2.50	4.50
Begonias	1.50	2.25	4.00
Black-Eyed Susan Vine	1.50	2.50	4.50
Bleeding Heart Vine	1.50	2.50	4.50
Chrysanthemum	1.75	2.50	4.50
Cyclamen	1.50	2.50	4.50
Daffodil	2.00	3.00	4.50
Easter Lily	2.00	3.00	4.50
Exacum	1.50	2.50	4.50
Fuchsia	1.50	2.50	4.50
Geraniums	1.50	2.50	4.50
Gloxina	2.00	4.00	5.50
Golden Candle	1.50	2.50	4.50
Hyacinth	2.00	3.50	5.00
Hydrangea	2.00	4.00	5.00

FLOWERING PLANTS *(continued)*	4"	6"	10"
Impatiens	1.50	2.50	4.50
Lantana	1.50	2.50	4.50
Orchids	3.00	4.50	7.00
Pocketbook Plant	1.50	2.25	4.00
Poinsettia	1.50	2.50	4.50
Primrose	1.50	2.50	4.50
Portulacas	1.50	2.50	4.50
Roses: Potted	2.00	4.00	5.50
Miniature	2.25	5.00	7.00
Tulips	2.00	4.00	5.00
Vinca	1.50	2.50	4.50

FRUIT-BEARING PLANTS	4"	6"	10"	14"
Avocado	1.50	3.00	5.50	12.50
Bananas	1.50	5.00	7.50	12.50
Citrus Trees	1.50	5.50	7.50	12.50
Edible Figs	1.50	5.50	7.50	10.00
Grapevines	2.00	3.00	5.50	10.00
Herbs	1.50	2.25	4.50	
Hot Peppers	1.50	2.25	4.50	
Kiwi Plants	2.50	4.50	6.50	
Papaya	1.50	2.50	4.50	12.50
Strawberries (potted)		2.50	4.50	
Sweet Peppers	1.00	2.00		4.00
Tarmarillo "Tree Tomato"		2.50	4.50	15.00
Tomatoes	1.00	2.00		4.00
Vegetable Assortments	1.00	2.00		4.00

LANDSCAPE PLANTS:
SHRUBS

	6"	10"		6"	10"
African Iris	1.75	4.75	Hibiscus (bush)	1.75	4.50
Allamanda	1.75	4.75	Ilex	1.75	4.50
Arborvitar	2.00	5.50	Ixora	1.75	4.50
Asparagus Fern	1.50	4.00	Junipers	1.75	4.25
Azaleas	2.00	4.50	Ligustrum	1.60	3.75
Bottlebrush	1.50	4.00	Liriope	1.75	4.25
Bougainvillea	2.00	5.00	Nandina	1.75	4.50
Begonias	1.50	4.00	Oleander	1.75	4.00
Confederate Jasmine	1.50	4.00	Pittosporum:		
Crape Myrtle	1.75	4.00	Green	1.60	4.00
Croton	2.00	5.00	Variegated	1.75	4.25
Heather	1.50	4.00	Wheeleri	1.75	4.25
Day Lilies	1.75	4.00	Podocarpus	2.00	5.50
Eleagnus	1.60	3.75	Society Garlic	1.60	4.00
Gardenia	2.75	7.50	Sterlitzia Regina/		
Ganzania	1.35	3.00	Bird of Paradise	3.00	7.50
Geranium	1.60	3.75	Viburnum	1.60	4.00

LANDSCAPE PLANTS: TREES		
	10"	14"
Bald Cypress	5.50	22.50
Bottlebrush		
Lanceolatus	5.00	20.00
Viminalis	5.50	22.50
Camphor	5.50	22.50
Golden Raintree	5.50	22.50
Ilex (Holly)		
East Palatka	7.00	25.00
Savannah	7.00	25.00
Ligustrum	5.50	22.50
Loquat	5.00	22.50
Magnolia	7.00	25.00
Oleander	5.00	20.00
Oak/Laurel	7.00	30.00
Pine/Slash	5.00	20.00
Red Cedar	5.00	22.50
Red Maple	5.00	22.50
Sweet Gum	5.00	22.50
Sycamore	5.00	22.50
Tallow	5.00	22.50
Wax Myrtle	4.00	20.00

Section 9
Delivery, Collecting, & Using Computers

Before shipping plants it is good to move them to a place where the shade is 50% more than where they were grown. Leave them there for two days to help them adjust to boxes and artificially lighted stores. Washing the soil thoroughly with water will also cut down on plant damage; do this two or three days before shipment. Place boxes in a cool, dry place after packaging. Experiment with the life of the plants in closed boxes. Most plants will last a week, but it is best for them not to be boxed for over 3 or 4 days.

Certain flowers and vegetable plants will do better in the summer under a light shade cloth, but probably will not need shade during the other seasons. Even with shade-grown foliage plants, shade may not be required in the winter.

If not enough shade cloth is used, plants may get a sunburn or dry out too fast. Too much shade will keep the plants from drying out sufficiently. A light meter can be used to adjust shade to the right degree. Most instruments come with a numbered guide. These meters are very easy to use. Just hold the meter away from direct light in the darkest area of the greenhouse. Your readings will vary depending on reflections and the direct point of sun.

By adjusting to a higher degree of shade you will get darker green foliage plants in most cases.

Some landscape plants grow better under a light shade cloth. There are also a couple of good shading paints on the market that turn clear during rains, then back to shade during sunny weather.

If you are growing hanging baskets in large volume (300 or more), hanging them high in the greenhouse close together (2' to 3' apart) can have a 55% to 75% shading effect.

Wood slats, log trims, and old lumber can be used as a lathing for a shade house.

The least expensive shade house I have found is constructed using 12' pressure-treated poles, aircraft cable and clamps, mobilehome anchors, and the appropriate size shade cloth to cover the top and sides. Poles are set about 20' apart at the corners, middle, and anywhere else needed. For strength, the aircraft cable is stretched over the top and then fastened to the ground with the mobilehome anchors. Then cover the structure with cloth and stitch it on at the corners and sides.

By growing your plants or just finishing them off under shade, they will be of higher quality. Most large buyers will try to find the local grower who uses shade in his growing operation. Sometimes this will be the only advertisement you'll need. Also, shade houses are a pleasant working area for noontime jobs.

PACKING AND LABELING

Any dirt on the leaves that is easily seen should be cleaned off all plants before packing. Excess dirt on pots should be wiped off with a wet cloth. Weak, brown leaves should be completely trimmed from the plant. Make sure that all leaves will support themselves if separated from other plants.

Plants that are sent out in large volume should be packed in cardboard boxes, preferably "live plant" boxes which can be bought through any large box company. The 23"x18"x 24" size is suitable for 6 to 8" hanging baskets and for 4½" or 6½" pots. For 4½" pots or 5" hanging baskets the 23"x 18"x 16" box is best. This will hold twenty 4½" pots or twelve 5" hanging baskets. All plants should be sleeved before packing in boxes. Paper sleeves are my favorite. The length is determined by the box size as well as the size of the pot. You will need 8"x 24" sleeves for 8" hanging baskets and 6"x 24" sleeves for 6" or 6½" pots.

TAGS

Be sure that all plants have individual tags with the name of the plant and care instructions. These can be purchased from one of the companies listed in Section 11. Also, it helps to include a letter-size piece of paper telling the store owner or employee how to care for the plants until they are sold. Usually the buyer will require that the outside of the box be labeled with your name, address, and phone number (along with their name). Get a rubber stamp or adhesive shipping labels for this purpose. Also, identify the contents of the box in the upper right hand corner of the box.

BOX CONSTRUCTION

Plants can do fine in boxes for a day or two before shipping if the tops are left open. This will allow a little light and air circulation. Boxes should be handled carefully after packing so that a minimum of soil is knocked out of the pots.

The boxes can be closed and fastened with a staple gun designed for this purpose, which can be purchased from your local box company. Place the bottom of the box on a homemade wooden frame, then staple at each flap. Staple the top down in the same manner. Use tape of a strong quality on the top, or use glue on the bottom of the box if desired.

After closing the boxes make sure they are well shaded. Direct sun on the outside of the box can create heat build-up inside. This can cause severe leaf damage if subjected to such heat for 3 or 4 hours.

Boxes should be at least 4" higher than the plants to allow adequate air circulation.

DELIVERY

Be sure to discuss transportation when making your sales. You might want to make deliveries personally at first. This can be easily done with a U-Haul truck or by renting a large tractor/trailer rig. Prices vary greatly, so shop around for the best deal. Get a refrigerated type trailer if you expect to haul more than a few hundred miles and if you have the quantity to warrant it.

You will be responsible for the plants until they are signed for at the point of delivery. Always get an official signature of acceptance.

Try to arrange for payment upon delivery. When starting out, the best way is to designate a

PAPER SLEEVES

SIZE	DIMENSIONS	PRICE PER 1000
4-18	5 - 13 - 18	$ 55.70
4-24	5 - 15-3/4 - 24	68.25
4-24 Azalea	6 - 12-1/2 - 24	63.15
4-30 Azalea	6 - 13-1/2 - 30	78.05
4-30 Poinsettia	6 - 13-1/2 - 30	78.05
5-18	6-1/2 - 14-1/2 - 18	57.95
5-24*	6-1/2 - 17 - 24	72.35
5-24 Poinsettia	8 - 12-3/4 - 24	66.55
5-30 Poinsettia	8 - 14 - 30	81.95
5-1/2-24 Lily	9 - 11-1/2 - 24	66.00
5-1/2-30 Lily	9 - 12-1/4 - 30	81.15
5-1/2-36 Lily	9 - 13-1/2 - 36	93.00
6-18	7- 14-3/4 - 18	59.05
6-24	7 - 17-1/2 - 24	73.20
6-24 Mum*	8-1/2 - 17 - 24	74.55
6-24 Tulip	9-1/2 - 14 - 24	70.05
6-30	6-1/2 - 19-1/2 - 30	91.50
6-30 Hydrangea	8-1/2 - 20-1/2 - 30	99.55
6-30 Lily	9-1/2 - 14 - 30	84.75
6-30 Mum*	8-1/2 - 19 - 30	94.10
6-30 Poinsettia	9 - 14-1/2 - 30	84.75
6-30 Tulip	9-1/2 - 15 - 30	87.05
6-36	6-1/2 - 22 - 36	109.00
6-36 Mum	8-1/2 - 21-1/4 - 36	111.45
6-36 Lily	9-1/2 - 14-1/2 - 36	93.35
6-36 Poinsettia	9 - 15-1/2 - 36	97.20
6-42 Poinsettia	9 - 16-1/2 - 42	118.25
7-24 Mum	9 - 17-3/4 - 24	76.30
7-30	9 - 20 - 30	96.25
7-36	9 - 22 - 36	114.00
7-42	9 - 24 - 42	139.30
7-42 Poinsettia	10 - 19-1/2 - 42	129.60
7-48 Poinsettia	10 - 20 - 48	149.25
8-30 Poinsettia	11-1/2 - 18 - 30	96.25
8-36 Poinsettia	11-1/2 - 19 - 36	110.70
8-42	11-1/2 - 24 - 42	145.55
8-42 Poinsettia	11-1/2 - 20-1/2 -42	140.55
8-48 Poinsettia	11-1/2 - 22-1/2 - 48	161.90
9-42	14 - 24 - 42	157.95
10-48	15 - 26 - 48	181.90
12-60	17 - 26 - 60	244.90
14-60	19 - 27 - 60	307.15
17-60	29 - 34 - 60	392.15
8-24 Hanging Basket	10-1/2 - 21-1/2 - 24	85.30
8-30 Hanging Basket	10-1/2 - 24-1/2 - 30	109.95
8-36 Hanging Basket	10-1/2 - 26 - 36	133.90
10-24 Hanging Basket	14-1/2 - 22-1/2 - 24	91.55
10-30 Hanging Basket	14-1/2 - 24 - 30	114.50
10-36 Hanging Basket	14-1/2 - 26 - 36	139.25

cash on delivery system. This is for your benefit until you have established your business and covered your initial investment in the plants. Also, until you have established your business on a regular order and delivery schedule it can save you costly delays in collection time. Most buyers will agree to this arrangement without hesitation.

After getting established and scheduling deliveries regularly, have a local motor line carry your plants to any part of the country. Ship F.O.B.; the buyer pays for all handling expenses also. The shipper (the motor line carrying the plants) is responsible from the moment he picks up the plants at your greenhouse. The shipper should promptly pay the grower for any damage that occurs in shipping.

Always inspect the plants again when you deliver them. Plants will react differently to long periods of darkness.

Stacking boxes on pallets inside the truck makes unloading large orders easier. Most warehouses have forklift operators to unload. Otherwise the boxes will have to be unloaded by hand.

BILLS OF LADING

A bill of lading should be filled out completely before the shipment leaves your nursery. This states the number of boxes, size, and destination. Sometimes a federal plant inspection stamp is required on the bill; your county agent can tell you when, where, and if you need it. The bill is then carried along with the plants to the buyer; it must be shown at weigh stations.

The bill of lading is signed when the plants are delivered. A copy is left with the buyer, another with the shipper, and one with the grower. This is your proof of delivery when billing by mail. Send an invoice as soon as delivery has been confirmed.

If payment is not received within 21 days, you might want to send a follow-up invoice. After 30 days you should telephone the buyer to check on payment. Have your copy of the bill of lading handy for questions the buyer may ask you regarding the shipment.

COLLECTING

The large grocery store chains usually pay within 21 to 30 days. In most cases smaller chains and locally owned stores pay within 10 to 15 days. You might want to offer a 1 or 2% discount if your invoice is paid within 10 days. This is usually to your advantage, and buyers also feel they are getting a bargain.

Be sure to check your buyer out thoroughly before extending credit. See if you can find someone else they have done business with and inquire about their credit standing and what limits they are allowed. You might also ask if they have ever had any payment problems. If they have, insist on C.O.D. (this is always the best system when first starting out).

If payment is not received promptly, call your buyer and verify the invoice to be sure an error was not made. In some cases a simple error on an invoice can delay payment.

The larger grocery chains and department stores sometimes send your invoice to a central office or accounts payable department. Track your bill down to the person responsible for paying, and inquire about their payment schedule. This way you should know to the day when to expect payment. If there is a problem, have them run it down and return your call that day.

The best way to ensure there is no delay is to double-check the address and amount of invoice before sending it out. It is good practice, when you have your invoices printed, to include a statement that all claims against damage must be made within 48 hours of receipt of shipment. Your invoices might also reference the 2% discount if paid in 10 days and 18% annual interest on unpaid balances over 30 days. This is an important system that will inspire fast payment.

STARTING WITH A SMALL BUSINESS COMPUTER

Micro or personal computers (PC's) make it economically possible for even very small businesses to acquire electronic data processing equipment. With its business applications, a microcomputer system gives you professional management planning and control capabilities that can maximize your personal management abilities and goals and your company's growth and profit performance. Use your best analysis and judgment when deciding on a computer for your business.

WHAT CAN COMPUTERIZING DO FOR YOU?

To answer this question, you must have a clear understanding of the long- and short-range goals of your firm, the advantages and disadvantages of alternatives to a computer, and what you specifically want to accomplish with a computer. Compare the best manual system you can develop using your present resources with the computer system you hope to get. It may be possible to improve your existing manual system and do the job effectively.

Generally, a business that is reasonably well organized and staffed will benefit from computerizing if it has large volumes of detailed or repetitious information that need to be handled with great speed and precision. A computer system can:

❖ *Organize and store many similarly structured pieces of information* (such as addresses for shipping labels)

❖ *Retrieve a single piece of information from many stored ones* (the address of a chain store)

❖ *Perform complicated mathematical computations quickly and accurately* (the terms of a loan amortized over many years)

❖ *Print information quickly and accurately* (sales reports, bills of lading, invoices)

❖ *Perform the same activity almost indefinitely and precisely the same way each time* (100 copies of a form letter, packing slips)

Managers use computers to solve many business problems. Some of the most common business applications are keeping transaction records (such as a Cash Receipts Journal, Receivables Ledger, and General Journal) and preparing statements and reports (such as a Balance Sheet, Income Statement, and Inventory Status Report).

Look at the following situations. These manual operations have areas that are usually improved by computerizing.

Accounts Receivable

Even if properly organized and maintained, a large volume of active accounts receivables can mean many hours spent posting sales and receipts and preparing statements. Unfortunately, as the volume of information increases, so does the number of errors.

Advertising

Using only manual systems, it is costly and complicated to have special sales programs directed toward particular customers. Manually prepared mass mailings are time-consuming and expensive.

Inventory

A large number of items or high volume turnover can mean numerous errors in tracking inventory. Errors in inventory control can result in lost sales and in unnecessarily high inventory levels of slow-moving products.

Payroll

Calculating and writing payroll checks are tedious manual operations. Also, it can be difficult to effectively implement any kind of employee incentive plan using manual procedures.

Planning

Manual systems make planning for the future time-consuming and difficult. *"What if?"* situations such as "If sales increase, to what extent will expenses increase?" are not easy to simulate with a manual system.

GENERAL BUSINESS APPLICATIONS

Business applications are available in packaged software programs that enable you to interact with the computer. General areas of computer applications are:

FINANCIAL MODELING programs prepare and analyze financial statements.

WORD PROCESSING programs compile statistics; plot trends and markets; and do market analysis, modeling, graphs, and forms.

CRITICAL PATH ANALYSIS programs divide large projects into smaller, more easily managed segments or steps, targeting goals and ultimate completion.

LEGAL PROGRAMS track cases and tap information from databases.

PAYROLL SYSTEM programs keep all payroll records; calculate pay, benefits, and taxes; and prepare paychecks.

AUTOMATED ENVIRONMENTAL CONTROL

The success of greenhouse operations hinges on the fact that crop after crop responds consistently to its environment. In recognizing the mechanistic relationship between a crop and its greenhouse environment, growers have increasingly come to rely on automatic control systems to provide consistent, favorable environmental conditions.

For example, in the recent past, it was common practice to manually water greenhouse crops. Today, most growers rely on automatic irrigation systems regulated by timers and solenoids. In addition to the labor-saving advantages, growers have realized that automated irrigation systems have horticultural advantages. They allow increased precision in regulating the timing of irrigation events and the amount of water that growers apply to their crops.

In the same manner, the trend from thermostats to electronic controllers has provided increased flexibility in regulating heaters, ventilation fans, and wet pads.

The next logical step is a computer-based greenhouse control system that can link and manage all of the automated control subsystems. Generally, computer-based control strategies can be much more sophisticated than other types of controllers. This provides the grower with more precise management capabilities for more efficient operation of heaters, ventilation fans, and other control equipment.

Less obviously, computerized control systems can help the development of a grower's overall management strategy by providing consistent, detailed data about the greenhouse environment.

Section 10
Guidelines to Organizing Your Business

Successful growers use many tools to achieve high profits in this industry. These businesses have learned the secret: *change*. Change involves many factors. One of them is seeing your employees as your greatest assets.

The growers who profit the most and grow steadily year after year are the ones who focus on communication with their employees. It is easy to forget this in the daily rush of getting things done, but it is imperative that you realize no amount of automation or management direction can match the powerful resources of your employees.

Pay attention to them. Encourage their ideas. Be directly involved with your staff every day by soliciting feedback, suggestions, and revisions. This is not meant as a way to "keep up appearances," but as real, "in the trenches" learning.

People are individuals with independent thoughts, actions, and abilities. It is up to the leadership within a company to tap into the knowledge of their employees and then use it. From a manager's standpoint, you have to give up to get. Relax tight controls and allow flexibility within the employee's job designation.

By giving priority to activities, explaining what goals you're after, and involving your employees, you become a team. You are working in harmony toward one objective.

Change also involves watching out for opportunity. By staying informed in the marketplace, you increase your chances of success. Good planning can be achieved through having information at your fingertips. Knowledge is power. The more you know about a project, the better your performance and likelihood of success.

Do your research. The information you gather is invaluable and guides you to the correct analysis of a problem, which then leads to a solution. Remember that in most things there is no absolute right or wrong, no "good" or "bad" answer. Flexibility is the key. It is your detailed, objective, joint effort of study with your people that points the way to superb achievement.

Change means being observant, absorbing, and listening. Find out what is going on around you as it pertains to your crop. Talk to employees, suppliers, competitors, and consumers. Get opinions about your business from all types of people. It might be painful at times, but it will help you see your company realistically instead of through rose-colored glasses.

Then follow through with their input. Make the changes necessary to improve customer relations or production levels; institute employee cutbacks; or diversify into other, compatible areas (sometimes change means learning to balance better). Identify where your company is heading and where you need improvement.

A one- to five- year business plan is an essential start. You need to stay on course, within reason. That means standing back occasionally and "taking stock." Every grower wanders from the path a bit, but it is important to stay on target for the most part.

Success may not always seem like success. Things that seem to go wrong or look like failures are priceless lessons needed to inspire thought, motion, and success. The more incidents of "incorrect" planning you experience will put you closer to your ultimate goal. The successful grower has made many more mistakes than an unsuccessful grower.

The secret is:

Do everything in the most economical way

Think a project through before starting it

Keep the thought fresh in mind for a forward, optimistic inspiration

This approach will be the driving force to accomplishing projects that take years to complete.

At the same time, try to succeed on at least one (smaller) project every day. Have more than one project going all the time, and think of little things you can complete daily. These will mount up to quite a nursery in no time at all. Like money in the bank, the larger your plant inventory, the larger your net worth.

LABOR REGULATIONS

State Employment Compensation Regulations
Dept. of Labor and Employment Security
Division of Unemployment Compensation
Employer Status Section
Bureau of Tax

Proof of Age - *If employment of minors is anticipated*
Dept. of Labor and Employment Security
Division of Labor, Employment & Training

Occupational Safety & Health Act (OSHA) - *For information and training on safety and health requirements and practices*
Dept. of Labor and Employment Security
Bureau of Industrial Safety and Health

Workers' Compensation Insurance - *Must be provided unless you qualify as a self-insured company*
Dept. of Labor and Employment Security
Division of Workers' Compensation
Bureau of Compliance

Carrier Practices & Benefits - *General inquiries*
Dept. of Labor and Employment Security
Bureau of Investigations

CONTROL OF THE BUSINESS

Sole Proprietorship
Gives you absolute authority over all business decisions.

Partnership
Control of the business is shared with your partners. This may lead to disputes. A partnership agreement could be helpful in solving pos-

sible disputes. However, you are still responsible for your partner's business actions along with your own.

Corporation (Standard or S)

Control depends on stock ownership. In other words, 51% stock ownership or control means you are able to make policy decisions. Control is exercised through regular board of directors' meetings and an annual stockholders' meeting. Records must be kept to document decisions made by the board of directors. Small, closely held corporations can operate more informally, but recordkeeping cannot be eliminated entirely. Officers of a corporation can be liable to stockholders for improper actions.

ORGANIZING YOUR BUSINESS

State

Corporate Filing and Fees (Standard or S)

These are to be filed only if your business is a corporation or if you plan to incorporate. Articles of incorporation must be prepared and executed in compliance with the "General Corporation Act" and delivered with the necessary fees and taxes to the Division of Corporations. Obtain appropriate forms from the Division of Corporations.

Name Availability

The Department of State will check to see if the name you wish to use for the corporation is available.

County

Fictitious Name Registration

If your business is not incorporated and you intend to use any name other than your own for business purposes, it must be registered under the Fictitious Name Act. Registration procedures include paying a service change in the county which is the principle place of business and giving notice of intent to use the business name by publication once a week for four weeks in a newspaper of general circulation in the county prior to registration.

Check with your County Clerk of the Circuit Court for specific registration procedures.

On-Site Considerations

Zoning Ordinances

Building Permits - City and/or County Authority

Covenants on Property - Property Owners or Developers

Topographic Maps & Soil Boring Reports - Property Owners or Developers

Flood-Prone Area Maps - U.S. Geological Survey

Permit to Connect a Private Drive -To a city street: City Engineer's Office. To a county road: County Roads Superintendent.

Permit to Discharge Waste - Into the atmosphere or waters of the state

Pollution Abatement System/Treatment Works - State permit required for operation

National Pollutant Discharge Elimination System (NPDES)

New Potable Water Supplies - Approval of plans

Municipal Water Supply Analysis - Requires periodic scanning by the water supplier

Permit to Dredge and Fill

Information on Regulations and Requirements - With respect to wastewater handling and pollution abatement systems

Solid Waste Law and Regulations - Obtain copy and comply with requirements

SELECT TYPE OF FINANCING

The need for capital to start and operate a business usually occurs in three stages: (1) to cover start-up costs, (2) to finance current operations (working capital), and (3) to expand the established business.

Starting Capital

Starting capital can be obtained in many ways. You may:

❖ Use personal savings.

❖ Borrow from friends, banks, or through the Small Business Administration.

❖ Borrow from life insurance policies.

❖ Mortgage residential real estate.

❖ Sell shares of stock to outside investors if you incorporate.

❖ Sell ownership to partners and employees.

❖ Obtain venture capital from public or private sources.

– Public sources include Small Business Investment companies (SBICs) and Minority Enterprise Small Business Investment companies.

– The majority of the private sources are either private individuals; wealthy families; private groups; or privately owned corporations, banks, and insurance companies.

Starting capital should be enough to cover living expenses for three months to a year, depending on the type of business. Some of the expenses to plan for are:

Rent and deposit
Starting inventory
Personal and employee salaries
Advertising, equipment, and repairs
Organizing costs
Insurance premiums
Taxes and license
Attorney and accounting fees
Management, consultant, and counseling fees
Utilities, telephone, and garbage removal

Working Capital

Many of the same sources used in start-up financing can also be used to gain additional working capital. In addition to the above sources, you may:

❖ Mortgage commercial or industrial real estate.

❖ Generate funds by good money management inside the business.

❖ Obtain trade credit from suppliers.

❖ Finance accounts receivable. Loans are made with the business's accounts receivable pledged as security.

❖ Factor accounts receivable. Your business's accounts receivable are sold to another firm.

❖ Borrow from commercial finance companies.

Expansion

Expanding a business usually requires a lot of capital. In addition to the sources listed under start-up and working capital, you may:

❖ Consider an equipment leaseback option. A business that already owns equipment can arrange a sale and leaseback agreement.

❖ Borrow from the Small Business Administration.

❖ Obtain financing through SBA 504-certified development companies.

❖ Use industrial revenue bond (IRB) financing.

❖ Borrow from community economic development corporations.

OBTAIN REQUIRED LICENSES AND PERMITS & REGISTER WITH APPROPRIATE AGENCIES

The following guidelines provide basic information you will need to begin any business with respect to initial licenses, permits, and registration requirements of local, state, and federal government agencies.

Federal

SS-4 Application for Employer Identification Number

When this form is properly completed and submitted to the Internal Revenue Service, it will register you with the Federal Government as a business. Unless you are a sole proprietor, registration is required even if you do not have employees. The form must be filed on or before the seventh day after the date on which business begins.

Ask for a copy of the Small Business Tax Kit for either sole proprietorship, general partnership, or a corporation. The IRS conducts workshops on the information contained in these kits.

City and County

Occupational Licenses

These are required for every business and are issued by counties and cities. You may need one or both, depending on your location. Check with the tax collector's office in your city and county to determine which licenses are required.

Certificate of Occupancy

After a business location has been selected, a certificate of occupancy must be obtained. Check with your city building inspection division to determine which forms are needed for your particular business.

Zoning Permits (Certificate of Use)

Check with your county planning department or building inspection division to determine which forms are needed for your particular business location.

OBTAIN NECESSARY FORMS FOR REPORTING TAXES AND OTHER REQUIREMENTS

Taxes on your business and other reporting requirements will depend on the nature of the business, its form of legal organization, and whether or not you have employees. Major federal, state, and local business taxes include:

Federal

940 Employer's Annual Unemployment Tax Return

Used to report and pay, on an annual basis, the federal unemployment compensation tax. If you have no employees, this form is not required.

941 Employer's Quarterly Federal Tax Return

Used to report, on a quarterly basis, the income tax and social security withheld from employee's wages and the social security matched by the employer.

County and City

City License and Tax - if required

City tax collector

County License and Tax - if required

County tax collector

State

UCS-1 Report to Determine Status

Used to determine if employer is liable for an unemployment compensation tax number.

UCT-65 Unemployment Compensation Tax Return

Used to report and pay quarterly employer's unemployment compensation tax based on employees' wages. This is paid to the State Unemployment Compensation Fund (not to be confused with workers' compensation insurance).

Dept. of Labor and Employment Security
Division of Unemployment Compensation

Workers' Compensation

If you have three or more employees, you are required to carry workers' compensation coverage.

Dept. of Labor and Employment Security
Division of Worker's Compensation
Bureau of Compliance

DR-1 Application for Certificate of Registration (Sales Tax Number)

Your state requires you to collect a retail sales tax on certain items; on the sale, resale, or lease of tangible personal property; and on the rental of real property. All businesses which collect the sales tax must secure a Certificate of Registration (sales tax number) from the Department of Revenue.

DR-15 Sales and Use Tax Report

Used to report and pay monthly the state sales tax collected.

DR-601-C Intangible Personal Property Tax Return

(Corporations and Partnerships)

DR-601-I Intangible Personal Property Tax Return

(Individual and Fiduciary)

Used to report and pay tax annually on intangible property such as accounts receivable, stocks and bonds, notes, and loans.

Corporate Income Tax

This is to be filed only if your business is a corporation or if you are planning to incorporate. General or limited partnerships are not subject to this tax unless one partner is a corporation, in which case a state partnership return may need to be filed.

The above forms may be obtained from:
Department of Revenue
Office of Taxpayer Assistance

Section 11
Plant Buyers & Suppliers

PLANT BUYERS

Listed below are the main headquarters of some of the largest buyers in the nation. Be sure to ask for the appropriate district produce or plant buyer for your area.

	# of stores		# of stores
Albertson's Grocery Boise, ID 208-344-3966	403	Kash & Karry Tampa, FL 813-621-0200	140
A & P Lakeland, FL 813-644-6388	397	K-Mart Dept. Stores East Brunswick, NJ 800-635-6278	1,865
Big Star Grocery Atlanta, GA 404-767-6735	55	McCory Dept. Stores York, PA 717-757-8181	1,200
Farmer Jack Grocery Detroit, MI 313-270-1000	76	Safeway Grocery, Inc. Oakland, CA 415-891-3000	1,321
I.G.A. Grocery St. Louis, MO 314-524-4000	2,243	Sears Dept. Stores Atlanta, GA 404-723-8480	1,051
Jewel Grocery Chicago, IL 708-531-6000	232	WalMart Dept. Stores Bentonville, AK 501-273-4000	1,537
J. C. Penney Dept. Store New York, NY 214-591-1000	1,479	Winn Dixie Grocery Jacksonville, FL 904-695-7800	611

SEED SUPPLIERS

Asgrow Seed Co.
1858 S. Dixie Ave.
Vero Beach, FL
407-562-2142

Ball Seed Co.
P.O. Box 335
W. Chicago, IL 60185
708-231-3500

Burgess Seed & Plant Co.
905 Four Season Rd.
Bloomington, IL 61701
309-663-9551

Crop King Inc.
P.O. Box 310
Medina, OH 44258
216-725-5656

Henry Field Seed & Nursery
Box 700
Shenandoah, IA 51602
712-246-2011

Flowery Branch Seeds
Box 1330
Flowery Branch, GA 30542
407-536-8380

Goldsmith Seeds
P.O. Box 1349
Gilroy, CA 95021
408-847-7333

Gurney's Seed & Nursery Co.
110 Capitol
Yankton, SD 57079
605-665-1671

Harris Seeds
60 Saginaw Dr.
Rochester, NY 14623
716-442-0410

Johnny's Selected Seeds
310 Foss Hill Rd.
Albion, ME 04910
207-437-4301

J. W. Jung Seed Co.
Randolph, WI 53956
414-326-3121

Liberty Seed Co. Inc.
Box 806-C9
New Philadelphia, OH 44663
216-364-1611

Henry F. Mitchell Co.
Church Rd.
King of Prussia, PA 19406
212-265-4200

Nichols Garden Nursery
1190 North Pacific Hwy.
Albany, OR 97321
503-928-9280

Northrup King Co.
7500 Olson Memorial Hwy.
Golden Valley, MN 55427
800-328-2420

Park Seed Co.
Greenwood, SC 29648-9983
800-845-3366

Premium Seed
915 E. Jefferson St.
Louisville, KY 40206
502-582-3897

Stokes Seeds Inc.
Box 548
Buffalo, NY 14240
416-688-4300

Thompson & Morgan
P.O. Box 1308A
Jackson, NJ 08527
908-363-2225

Twilley Seeds
P.O. Box 65
Trevose, PA 19047
215-639-8000

W. Atlee Burpee Co.
300 Park Ave
Worminster, PA 18974
215-674-4915

Willhite Seed Co.
P.O. Box 23
Poolville, TX 76076
817-599-8656

WHOLESALE NURSERIES

Abbott-IPCO Inc. P.O. Box 551329 Dallas, TX 75355	214-341-1585	*caladium bulbs*
Brier's Greenhouses P.O. Box 326 Rockwood, TN 37854	615-354-9765	*cacti, succulents*
Carter's Greenhouse Box 223 Rockwood, TN 37854	615-354-1093	*bare-rooted scheffleras, neanthe bella palms*
Casa Flora Box 8427 Dallas, TX 75205	800-233-3376	*diffenbachia & fern liners*
Colorado Cutting Inc. P.O. Box 337 Lafayette, CO 80026	303-665-5725	*annuals, perennials, herbs, ground covers*
Davidson-Wilson Greenhouses Route #2 Box 168 Crawfordsville, IN 47933	317-364-0556	*geraniums, African violets*
Dutch Hill Growers Monroe, NC 28110	800-359-7659	*Gerber's daisy plugs*
Paul Ecke Ranch Box 488 Encinitas, CA 92024	619-753-1134	*New Guinea impatiens cuttings, poinsettia cuttings & plugs*
Epp's Greenhouses Inc. Embleton Rd., Huttonville Ontario, Canada LOJ - 180	416-455-8486	*tissue culture, Boston fern liners*
Flowerwood Wholesale Greenhouse P.O. Box 217 Crystal Lake, IL 60014	815-455-2220	*New Guinea impatiens*
Greenbriar Nurseries Inc. 2025 NE 70th Street Ocala, FL 32670	904-351-3664	*hardy woody ornamentals*
Holtkamp Greenhouses Inc. P.O. Box 8158 Nashville, TN 37207	800-443-2290	*African violet liners*

WHOLESALE NURSERIES *(continued)*

Inglis Greenhoues Inc. 6613 Southern Blvd. Youngstown, OH 44512	216-758-3545	*rooted & unrooted geraniums*
Johnson International P.O. Box 46 Marlboro, MA 01752	508-562-2516	*30 varieties of geraniums, rooted & unrooted cuttings*
Jolly Farmer Nursery Route 10 E. Lempster, NH 03605	800-695-8300	*plugs, annuals, and cydamen; geranium cuttings*
L&L Liner Nursery Route #2 Box 103 Wauchula, FL 33873	813-773-6989	*woody ornamental specialist*
Langeveld Bulb Co. 317 Fairfield Rd. Freehold, NJ 07728	800-526-0467	*largest grower & importer of bulbs from Holland, over 300 varieties*
New England Mum Box 700 Sorrento, FL 32776	904-383-2433	*rooted and unrooted, 75 varieties of mums*
Nor East Miniature Roses 58 Hammond Rowley, MA 01961	800-426 6485	*miniature roses*
Oglesby Plant Lab Inc. Route #2 Box 9 Altha, FL 32421	800-327-3812	*tissue cultures, microcuttings*
Oregon Lily Company 15676 Hwy. 101 South Brookings, OR 97415	800-253-4411	*Easter lily bulbs*
Park Seed Wholesale Cokesbury Rd. Greenwood, SC 29647	800-845-3366	*vegetable & flowering plant liners*
Phyton Technologies Inc. 7325 Oak Ridge Hwy. Knoxville, TN 37931	615-690-9988	*foliage plugs & tissue cultures*
Pleasant View Gardens RFD #3, Box 3701 Pittsfield, NH 03263	800-343-4784	*plugs & cell pack liners*

WHOLESALE NURSERIES (continued)

Frank Smith & Sons 876 Indian Trail Rd. Carleton, MI 48117	313-654-8200	*bedding plant plugs*
Speedling Inc. P.O. Box 238 Sun City, FL 34268	800-426-4400	*annual & perennial liners*
Springbrook Gardens Inc. 6776 Heisley Rd. P.O. Box 388 Mentor, OH 44061	216-255-3059	*field-grown perennials, over 1000 varieties*
Sullivan's Nursery 1000 Round Lake Rd. Mount Dora, FL 32757	800-344-6982	*landscaping plants (4" to 30-gal.), 65 acres production*
Sun Bulb Co. Inc. P.O. Box 698 Arcadia, FL 33821	813-494-4022	*flower bulbs, orchid starter kits*
H. R. Talmage & Sons 36 Sound Avenue, RFD #1 Riverhead, NY 11901	516-727-0124	*nearly finished geraniums, 4-1/2", buy 1500 get 1575*
Thorobred Trees Inc. P.O. Box 5189 Ocala, FL 32678	904-533-3665	*80 acres of trees, over 30 varieties*
Ulery Greenhouse Co. P.O. Box 1108 Springfield, OH 45501	800-722-2959	*begonia plugs*
Windmill Farms Nurseries Rt. #1, Box 156 Zolfo Springs, FL 33890	813-735-0904	*liner propagation, over 150 varieties*
Yoder Brothers P.O. Box 230 Barberton, OH 44203	800-321-9573	*cuttings, plugs, brokers, foliage, annuals, perennials*

GREENHOUSES

Atlas Greenhouse Systems
Rt 1, Box 339
Alapaha, GA 31622
800-346-9902

Crop King Inc.
P.O. Box 310
Medina, OH 44528
216-725-5656

D.A.C.E., Inc.
1937 High St.
Longwood, FL 32750
407-321-7771

Dixie Greenhouse Mfg. Co.
Rt. 1 Box 339
Alapala, GA 31622
800-346-9902

Gardener's Supply Co.
128 Intervale Rd.
Burlington, VT 05401
800-863-1700

Ludy Greenhouses Mfg. Corp
P.O. Box 141
New Madison, OH 45346
800-255-5839

Structures Unlimited
2122 Whitfield Park Ave.
Sarasota, FL 34243
813-756-8129

U.S. Systems Inc.
7 East 12th Street
St. Cloud, FL 34769
407-892-4521

GREENHOUSE EQUIPMENT

ACME Engineering Equipment Box 978 Muskogee, OK 74402	918-682-7791	*fans, shutters, rootcells*
Agrifim 1279 W. Moraga Fresno, CA 93711	209-431-20037	*drip systems*
Agritech P.O. Box 577 Broadway, NC 27505	919-258-9113	*watering & fog systems*
Automatic Equipment Mfg. Co. 1 Mill Rd. Pender, NE 68047	402-385-3051	*mist blowers*
Brighton By-Product Co., Inc. P.O. Box 23 New Brighton, PA 15066	800-245-3502	*shade cloth*
Cravo Equipment Whiteswan Rd. Rt. 1 Brantford, Ontario Canada N3T5L4	519-759-8226	*shading systems*

GREENHOUSE EQUIPMENT (continued)

Crop King Inc. P.O. Box 310 Medina, OH 44258	216-725-5656	*hydroponic systems, fans, heaters, poly film, control systems*
Datasphere/Doane Info. Serv. 6443 S.W. Beaverton Hwy., #305 Portland, OR 97221	503-297-9035	*computer software & hardware*
H. C. Davis & Sons Mfg. Co., Inc. Box 395 Bonner Springs, KS 66012	913-422-3000	*soil mixing machines*
FVG America, Inc. 8700 Xylon Ave. Minneapolis, MN 55445	800-451-4016	*poly covering*
Feaster Horticultural Corp. 84 Spoonbill Lane Ellenton, FL 34222	813-729-4900	*conveyers & heaters*
W. W. Grainger, Inc. 6725 Todd Blvd. Seattle, WA 98188	206-251-5030	*fans, motors, hardware*
Gravely International 1 Gravely Lane Clemmons, NC 27012	919-766-4721	*utility tractors*
Imperial Builders & Supplies P.O. Box 670 Apopka, FL 32703	407-889-4147	*heaters & fans*
Infared Systems 1719 Old Highway 99 South Mt. Vernon, WA 98273	206-424-5900	*growth zone heaters*
Irrigation World, Inc. 887 Apopka-Ocoee Rd. Apopka, FL 32704	407-886-7374	*drip irrigation*
Javo USA, Inc. 1900 Albritton Dr., Suite GH Kennesaw, GA 30144	404-428-4491	*soil mixing & filling machines*

GREENHOUSE EQUIPMENT *(continued)*

Leinbachs, Inc. 4995 Reynolds Rd. Winston-Salem, NC 27106	919-924-6933	*mist blowers*
Maxi Products Co. Inc. 2536 Center Ave Jamesville, WI 53545	608-755-1199.	*dump truck & trailer bodies*
MEE Industries, Inc. 4443 N. Rowland Ave. El Monte, CA 91731	818-350-4180	*fog systems*
Microjet Irrigation Systems P.O. Box 620519 Orlando, FL 32862	407-857-0011	*irrigation systems*
Nelson Irrigation Corp. Route 1 Box 1141 Newberry, FL 32669	904-472-3323	*irrigation systems*
Poly-Tex, Inc. P.O. Box 458 Castle Rock, MN 55010	800-852-3443	*poly-vent greenhouse side curtains*
Rain Bird Sales, Inc. 145 N. Grand Avenue Glendora, CA 91740	818-914-7361	*irrigation*
Reznor Heating McKinley Avenue Mercer, PA 16137	412-662-4400	*heaters*
Rite-Flo Supply 4909 W. Hanna Avenue Tampa, FL 33684	813-884-7535	*irrigation systems*
Roberts Irrigation Products 700 Rancheros Drive San Marcos, CA 92069	619-744-4711	*irrigation systems*
Rough Brothers P.O. Box 16010 Cincinnati, OH 45216	800-543-7351	*rolling benches, heating systems*

GREENHOUSE EQUIPMENT (continued)

Rounhouse Box 1744 Cleveland, TX 77328	713-593-1118	*shade houses*
X. S. Smith Inc. Drawer X Red Bank, NJ 07701	800-631-2226	*benches*
Speedy Seeders, Inc. W119 12th County Hwy. V Lodi, WI 53555	800-255-5021	*seeders*
Structural Plastics Corp 2750 Lippincott Blvd. Flint, MI 48507	800-523-6899	*tables & benches*
Sunderman Mfg. Co. Route 1 Box 14 Baltic, SD 57003	605-529-5470	*heaters*
Valcon 10837 Central Avenue El Monte, CA 91733	818-444-5466	*irrigation controls*

MISCELLANEOUS WHOLESALE SUPPLIERS

Agra Tech Inc 2131 Piedmont Way Pittsburg, CA 94565	415-432-3399	*miscellaneous*
Agri-Carts Mfg. Inc. P.O. Box 40 Mascotte, FL 34736	904-429-4740	*handcarts*
American Claywork & Supply 857 Bryant St. Denver, CO 80204	303-534-4044	*containers*
Arbico Inc. P.O. Box 4247 Tucson, AZ 85738	800-767-2847	*biological control, beneficial insects*

MISCELLANEOUS WHOLESALE SUPPLIERS (continued)

Atlas Peat & Soil P.O. Box 867 Boynton Beach, FL 33435	305-734-7300	*potting mixes*
Berthoud Sprayers 3783 Pipestone Rd. Sodus, MI 49126	616-925-1871	*spraying equipment*
B&K Installations 246 SW 4th Ave. Homestead, FL 33030	800-523-3870	*miscellaneous*
B.F.G. Supply Co. 14500 Kinsman Rd. Burton, OH 44021	800-321-0608	*rockwool, plant sleeves, shading compound*
Charley's Greenhouse Supply 1569 Memorial Mt. Vernon, WA 98273	206-428-2626	*miscellaneous*
Chemical Containers P.O. Box 1307 Lake Wales, FL 33859	813-638-1407	*water testing*
Cookson Pottery, Inc. 48 Potters Lane Roseville, OH 43777	614-697-7307	*containers*
Crofton Growers Supply 7641 Vantage Way, Suite 208 Delta, B.C. Canada V4G1A6	604-946-5641	*miscellaneous*
Crop King Inc. P.O. Box 310 Medina, OH 44258	216-725-5656	*media, fertilizer injectors, poly lock, consulting services*
D&L Grower Supply 546 B E. 28th Div. Hwy Litity, PA 17543	717-627-6737	*miscellaneous*
DWF Greenhouse Supply 4800 Dahlia St. Denver, CO	800-829-8280	*miscellaneous supplies; water, soil, & tissue testing*
Economy Label Sales, Inc. P.O. Box 350 Daytona Beach, FL 32015	~~800-874-7020~~	*tags*

MISCELLANEOUS WHOLESALE SUPPLIERS (continued)

Fafard Soils P.O. Box 3190 Springfield, MA 01101	413-786-4343	*potting mixes*
Falcon Growers Supply, Inc 2601 W. Orange Blossom Trail Apopka, FL 32712	407-886-8118	*miscellaneous*
Farm Supply Co. of Cornelia P.O. Box 826 Cornelia, GA 30531	404-778-8522	*shade cloth*
Gage Industries, Inc. P.O. Box 1318 Lake Oswego, OR 97035	503-639-2177	*containers*
Gardener's Supply Co. 128 Intervale Rd. Burlington, VT 05401	800-863-1700	*all-natural pest control, beneficial insects, organic fertilizers, Roots® organic soil treatment, APS-24, mushroom spores*
E. C. Geiger Co. Route 63, Box 285 Harleysville, PA 19438	215-256-6511	*miscellaneous*
Gerhart, Inc. 6346 Avon Belden Rd. North Ridgeville, OH 44039	216-327-8056	*beneficial insects*
W. R. Grace & Co. 62 Whittmore Ave. Cambridge, MA 02140	617-876-71400	*potting mixes*
Growers Systems, Inc. 2950 North Weil St. Milwaukee, WI 53212	414-263-3131	*growing trays & conveyors, Vandana seeders*
Hydro-Gardens Inc. P.O. Box 9707 Colorado Springs, CO 80932	719-495-2266	*irrigation systems & hydraulics*
IEM Plastics P.O. Box 1975 Reidsville, NC 27323-1975	800-222-7564 919-342-0356	*containers*
Jiffy Products of America, Inc. 1119 Lyon Rd. Batavia, IL 60510	800-323-1047	*potting mixes*

MISCELLANEOUS WHOLESALE SUPPLIERS (continued)

Lerio Corp.
P.O. Box 2084
Mobile, AL 36652 *1/27) w/seal* 205-457-7661 *containers*

Master Tag
9350 Walsh Rd.
Montague, MI 49437 800-253-0439 *plant tags*

Mellinger's
2370 Range Rd.
N. Lima, OH 44452 216-549-9861 *miscellaneous*

Midwest Growers Supply
918 Paramount Pkwy.
Batavia, IL 60510 708-879-1300 *miscellaneous*

Micro Vane, Inc.
8135 Coxs Drive
Kalamazoo, MI 49002 800-222-0677 *software*

O. S. Plastic, Inc.
3091 Holcomb Bridge Rd., #M2
Norcross, GA 30071 404-448-7701 *containers & sleeves*
Debbie 1800-241-9241 FAX 404-448-7705

Plastomer, Inc.
P.O. Box 14000
Ontario, Canada L4M4V3 705-726-0225 *plastics*

Pam Pottery
8880 N.W. 15th St.
Miami, FL 33172 305-592-5575 *clay pots*

Solo Inc.
P.O. Box 5030
Newport News, VA 23605 804-245-4228 *backpack sprayers*

Speeding Inc.
P.O. Box 7238
Sun City, FL 33586 813-645-3221 *miscellaneous*

Strickland Peat Co., Inc.
7219 Strickland Lane
Keystone Heights, FL 32656 904-473-7109 *potting mixes*

Stuppy Inc.
P.O. Box 12456
N. Kansas City, MO 64116 800-877-5025 *irrigation controls*

MISCELLANEOUS WHOLESALE SUPPLIERS (continued)

T.L.C. Polyform Inc. 13055 15th Ave. N Plymouth, MN 55441	612-542-2240	*containers*
Visqueen Film Products 1100 Boulders Pkwy. Richmond, VA 23225	804-330-1000	*poly film*
Wetsel Seed Company, Inc. P.O. Box 791 Harrisonburg, VA 22801	703-434-6753	*miscellaneous*
Worm's Way 3151 South Highway 446 Bloomington, IN 47401	812-331-0300	*hydroponic equipment, grow lights, fertilizer*

ROCKWOOL HYDROPONICS EQUIPMENT

Agro-Dynamics, Inc. 7950 E. Prentice Ave. Englewood, CO 80111 303-220-0585	Gro-Prod. Inc. 1078 Rt. 46 Clifton, NJ 07013 201-614-8834	Sharp and Son, Inc. 900 Lind Ave. SW Renton, WA 98055 206-235-4510
Crop King, Inc. P.O. Box 310 Medina, OH 44258 216-725-5656	Hydro-Gardens, Inc. P.O. Box 9707 Colorado Springs, CO 95131 800-634-6362	Worm's Way 3151 S. Highway 446 Bloomington, IN 47401 812-331-0300 *(also in MA, FL, & MO)*

SOIL, PLANT & WATER ANALYSIS

A&L Laboratories
1010 Carver Rd.

Modesto, CA 95350	209-529-4080
Lubbock, TX	806-763-4278
Memphis, TN	901-527-2780
Fort Wayne, IN	219-483-4759
Omaha, NB	402-334-7770
Richmond, VA	804-743-9401
Pompono Beach, FL	305-972-3255

Fisons Analytical Lab
177 San Fordville Rd.
Warwick, NY 10990
914-986-6667

J. M. McConkey and Co.
P.O. Box 1690
Sumner, WA 98390
206-863-8111

TRADE MAGAZINES & ASSOCIATIONS

American Greenhouse Vegetable Growers
P.O. Box 20228
Columbus, OH 43220
719-531-0505

American Horticultural Society
7931 E. Blvd. Drive
Alexandria, VA 22308
703-768-5700

The Business of Herbs
RR2, Box 246
Shevlin, MN 56676
218-657-2478

Florida Foliage Magazine & Association
57 East 3rd St.
Apopka, FL 32703
407-886-1036

Foliage Marketing Institute
RR 1 Box 1115
Boynton Beach, FL 33437
407-966-8855

Greenhouse Grower Magazine
37841 Euclid Ave.
Willoughby, OH 44094
216-942-2000

Grower Talks Magazine
P.O. Box 532
Geneva, IL 60134
708-208-9080

Hobby Greenhouse Association
8 Glenn Terrace
Bedford, MA 01730

Hydroponic Society of America
P.O. Box 6067
Concord, CA 94524
510-682-4193

Produce Marketing Assoc.
P.O. Box 6036
Newark, DL 19714-6036
302-738-7100

Tissue Culture Assoc.
8815 Centre Park Drive
Columbia, MD 21045
301-992-0946

Wholesale Nursery Growers of America
1250 I Street NW, Suite 500
Washington, D.C. 20005
202-789-2900

U.S. COOPERATIVE EXTENSION SERVICE

Broken down by headquarters
of the Extension Service for each state

Write to the main office in your state for helpful literature on your type of crop. Also, ask for a list of the publications that are available, and for information on soil testing.

ALABAMA
Auburn University
Auburn, AL 36830

ALASKA
University of Alaska
Fairbanks, AK 99701

ARIZONA
University of Arizona
Tucson, AZ 85721

ARKANSAS
P.O. Box 391
Little Rock, AR 72203

CALIFORNIA
University of California
2200 University Ave.
Berkeley, CA 94720

COLORADO
Colorado State University
Fort Collins, CO 80521

CONNECTICUT
University of Connecticut
Storrs, CT 06268

DELAWARE
University of Delaware
Newark, DE 19711

DISTRICT OF COLUMBIA
Federal City College
1424 K. Street, NW
Washington, D.C. 20005

FLORIDA
University of Florida
Gainesville, FL 32611

GEORGIA
University of Georgia
Athens, GA 30601

HAWAII
University of Hawaii
Honolulu, HI 96822

IDAHO
University of Idaho
Morrill Hall
Moscow, ID 83843

ILLINOIS
University of Illinois
Urbana, IL 61801

INDIANA
Purdue University
Lafayette, IN 47907

IOWA
Iowa State University
Ames, IA 50010

KANSAS
Kansas State University
Manhattan, KS 66506

KENTUCKY
University of Kentucky
Lexington, KY 40506

LOUISIANA
Louisiana State University
Baton Rouge, LA 70803

MAINE
University of Maine
Orono, ME 04473

MARYLAND
University of Maryland
College Park, MD 20742

MASSACHUSETTS
University of Massachusetts
Amherst, MA 01002

MICHIGAN
Michigan State University
East Lansing, MI 48823

MINNESOTA
University of Minnesota
St. Paul, MN 55101

U.S. COOPERATIVE EXTENSION SERVICE
(continued)

MISSISSIPPI
Mississippi State University
309 University Hall
Mississippi State, MS 39762

MISSOURI
University of Missouri
309 University Hall
Columbia, MO 65201

MONTANA
Montana State University
Bozeman, MT 59715

NEBRASKA
University of Nebraska
Lincoln, NE 68508

NEVADA
University of Nevada
Reno, NV 89507

NEW HAMPSHIRE
University of New Hampshire
Talor Hall
Durham, NH 03824

NEW JERSEY
Rutgers — The State University
P.O. Box 231
New Brunswick, NJ 08903

NEW MEXICO
New Mexico State University
Las Cruces, NM 88001

NEW YORK
New York State College
  of Agriculture
Ithaca, NY 14853

NORTH CAROLINA
North Carolina State University
Raleigh, NC 27607

NORTH DAKOTA
North Dakota State University
Fargo, ND 58102

OHIO
Ohio State University
2120 Fyffe Rd.
Columbus, OH 43210

OKLAHOMA
Oklahoma State University
Stillwater, OK 74074

OREGON
Oregon State University
Corvallis, OR 07331

PENNSYLVANIA
Pennsylvania State University
University Park, PA 16802

PUERTO RICO
University of Puerto Rico
Rio Piedras, Puerto Rico 00928

SOUTH CAROLINA
Clemson University
Clemson, SC 29631

SOUTH DAKOTA
South Dakota State University
Brookings, SD 57006

TENNESSEE
University of Tennessee
P.O. Box 1071
Knoxville, TN 37901

TEXAS
Texas A&M University
College Station, TX 77848

UTAH
Utah State University
Logan, UT 84321

VIRGIN ISLANDS
P.O. Box 166 Kingshill
St. Croix, Virgin Islands 00850

VIRGINIA
Virginia Polytechnic
Institute and State University
Blacksburg, VA 24061

WASHINGTON
Washington State University
Pullman, WA 99163

WEST VIRGINIA
West Virginia University
294 Coliseur
Morgantown, WV 99163

WISCONSIN
University of Wisconsin
432 North Lake Street
Madison, WI 53706

WYOMING
University of Wyoming
Box 3354
University Station
Laramie, WY 82070

Suggested Reading

All books can be located by finding the publisher's name and contacting them. They will be listed in a book at your public library called <u>Books in Print</u>.

How to Build Greenhouses - Sun Houses. Donald R. Brann. ISBN-0-87733-0011-5, $5^{95} (paperback ISBN-0-87733-611-3, $4^{50}) EASI BILD.

Carbon Dioxide Enrichment of Greenhouse Crops: Status & Carbon Dioxide Sources. Herbert Z. Enoch & Bruce A. Kimball. 2 volumes, 208 pages, ISBN -0-8193-5610-5, CRC PR, $218.

Diseases of Greenhouse Plants. J. T. Fletcher. ISBN-0-582-44263-X.

Gardening Under Cover: A Northwest Guide to Solar Greenhouses, Cold Frames & Cloches. William Head. ISBN-0-912365-23-4, Satquach Bks.

Light Transmission & Photosynthesis in Greenhouses. T. and Goudriann J. Kozai. ISBN-90-220-0646-8, Unipub, $8^{50}.

Greenhouse Management: Guide to Structures, Environmental Control, Materials Handling, Crop Programming & Business Analysis. Robert W. Langhans. ISBN-0-9604006-2-1, Halcyon Ithaca, $30.

Commercial Flower Forcing, 8th Edition. Alex Laurie. ISBN-0-07-036633-0, McGraw, $49^{95}.

A Solar Greenhouse Guide for the Pacific Northwest. Tim Magee. ISBN-0-934478-26-0, Ecotape, $6.

A Solar Greenhouse Guide for Flower and Plant Production. Kennard S. Nelson. ISBN-0-8134-2070-9, 2070, Inter Print Pubs, $26.

Nursery & Greenhouse Mechanization Equipment & Manufacturers, revised edition. Paperback, C1184, Am. Soc. Ag. Eng., $12^{75}.

Greenhouse Grow How. John H. Pierce. ISBN-0-918730-01-5, MacMillan, $19^{95}.

Master Guide to Planning Profitable Hydroponic Greenhouse S-CEA Operations. Adam J. Savage. ISBN-0-934495-02-5, $50.

The Homeowner's Complete Handbook for Add-On Solar Greenhouses and Sunspaces. Andrew M. Shapiro. ISBN-0-87857-507-3, $19^{95}.

Plastic Greenhouses for Warm Climates. Kjell Virhammar. Paperback, ISBN-92-5-101168-0, Unipub, $9.

The Complete Book of the Greenhouse. Ian Walls. ISBN-0-7063-6653-0, Trafalagar Sq-David and Charles, $34^{95}.

Scientific Greenhouse Gardening. P. K. Willmott. EP Pub, England, $40.

Sun Rooms: Create a Beautiful Enclosed Glass Extension for Your Home. Cheri R. Wolpert. ISBN-0-89586-738-9, HP Books, $24^{95}.

Exotic Plant Manual. A. B. Graf. ISBN-0911266-13-5, MacMillan.

Foliage Plant Production. Jasper N. Joiner. ISBN-0-13-322867-3-P-H.

Hydroponic Food Production. Howard M. Resh. ISBN-0-88007-171-0, Woodbridge Press.

Plants From Test Tubes. Lidiane Kyte. ISBN-0-88192-040-1, Timber Press.

Profitable Garden Center Management. Louis Berninger. ISBN-0-8359-5633-4, Reston Publishers.

Rodale's Illustrated Encyclopedia of Herbs. Robert Rodale. ISBN-0-87857-699-1, Rodale Press.

Ball Red Book. Vic Ball. 720 pages, Capability Books, $51^{95}.

The Commercial Greenhouse. James Boodley. ISBN-0-8273-1718-2, Delmar Press.

The Herb Book. John Lust. ISBN-0-553-2-6770-1, Bantam.

Tropica; Color Cyclopedia of Exotic Plants. A. B. Graf. ISBN-0-68415568-0, MacMillan.

Greenhouse Operation and Management. 4th edition by Paul V. Nelson. A complete, up-to-date guide to profitable greenhouse operation. Includes a discussion of the floricultural market, its changes and directions, and new means of distribution. Covers greenhouse construction, heating and cooling, rooting media, watering, fertilization, use of carbon dioxide, light and temperature, chemical growth regulation, insect and disease control, post-production handling, marketing, and business management. Invaluable! 598 pages. $53^{50}

Diseases and Pests of Ornamental Plants. 5th edition by Pascal P. Pirone. Up-to-date methods for controlling diseases, mites, and insects on over 500 genera of ornamental plants. Excellent reference for greenhouse, garden center, or nursery. $45^{50}

Bedding Plants III. A Penn State University manual. Covers the entire range of the bedding plant industry, including seeds, germination, seedlings, culture, production practices, flowers and vegetables, structures, equipment, systems, disease, insects, weed and air pollution problems, economics, marketing, and management. Well illustrated with drawings, pictures, tables. Paperback, 560 pages. $26^{95}

Seed-Propagated Geraniums. Allan M. Armitage. A complete discussion of the whys and hows of production of hybrid seed geraniums. Deals with cultivars, culture, pests, diseases, costs, and future trends. For both beginning growers and veterans alike. A valuable handbook for the better production of an important crop. 44 pages. $9^{95}

Fruits and Vegetables of the World. John Goode and Carol Wilson. An invaluable reference which includes notes on identification, origin, description, taste, and availability of the world's fruits and vegetables; advice on use and preparation; and hundreds of fascinating recipes. 205 pages, 100 illustrations, 8 color photos, 0-8509-300-4. $19^{95}

Fuchsia Culture. American Fuchsia Society, Ed. Fuchsias are not only flowers of great beauty, but they also require a special quality of care to stay healthy and vibrant. This easy-to-read text includes complete information on identification, soil, pests and diseases, hybridizing and registration, climates, and indoor growing. 160 pages, 21 illustrations, 96 color photos, 0-9613167-1-3. $9^{95}

Growing Houseplants in Temperate and Cool Climates. Ross James. Covers watering, feeding, repotting, hanging baskets, propagation, greenhouses, ferneries, pests and diseases, plant selection and plant life, color, light, heat, and humidity in the home. Includes a quick reference table for propagation temperature, light, watering requirements, and flowering times. 176 pages, color photos, 0-85091-287-3. $16^{95}

Growing Media for Ornamental Plants and Turf. K. A. Handreck & N. D. Black. A guide to the production and management of specialized growing media in which plants are grown. Topics include the selection of materials for potting mixes, fertilizers, efficient use of water, drainage, salinity, disease prevention, and the preparation of soils for landscape planting. Cloth, 401 pages, 262 photos/illustrations/charts, 0-86840-177-3. $29⁹⁵

Growing Trees for Farms, Parks & Roadsides: A Revegetation Manual. Julianne Venning. Practical advice on tree planting, using a wide range of cost-effective techniques. Includes step-by-step procedures: planning, selecting species, collecting seed, preparing the site, and site maintenance. The author, an expert in revegetation, discusses planting by seedlings, direct seeding, and natural regeneration featuring case studies, ecological concerns, extensive research, and seed and material suppliers. Paperback, 126 pages, 14 color photos, 0-85091-273-3. $19⁹⁵

How to Propagate Plants. Jack Plumridge. Compete, accurate, and easy to understand, this book covers every aspect of propagating plants. It gives examples and clearly details the advantages and disadvantages of each method of propagation. Paperback, 224 pages, 16 pages color, 0-85091-243-1. $12⁹⁵

Hydroponics for Everyone: A Practical Guide to Gardening in the 21st Century. Dr. Struan Sutherland. A home hydroponics guide which caters to everyone—from simple one-container, non-recycling systems to more comprehensive and complex hydroponic set-ups. This book is easy to understand, and is supplemented with diagrams, tables, and photographs. Paperback, 120 pages, 0-908090-94-3. $17⁹⁵

Modern Plant Propagation. Allan Gardiner. Covers all propagation techniques and skills with step-by-step diagrams, giving details of propagation for a comprehensive alphabetical list of plants. There are sections on soil mediums, uses of root-promoting substances, post-propagation care, and the latest equipment innovations. Paperback, 176 pages, 0-85091-283-0. $16⁹⁵

Glossary

acclimatize – The process of moving plants to shade so growing conditions of final destination won't shock the plants.

acid – Acid conditions exist when pH of a solution is below 7.0.

alkaline – Alkaline conditions exist when pH of a solution is higher than 7.0.

ammonium toxicity – A physiological disorder of plants which arises due to the presence excessive ammonium forms of nitrogen in the soil. Signs are scorching of leaf margins and loss of roots.

annual – A plant which completes its life cycle and dies after the end of one growing season.

asexual – Without sex, vegetative.

axil – The point of attachment of lateral growth to the stem.

bedding plants – Plants used in flower beds.

biennial – A plant that requires two years to complete its cycle.

bulb – A thickened bud, usually underground, capable of producing a new plant. Also, a fleshy tuber or corm that resembles a bulb.

cell culture – The culture of single cells, often included in the broad term "tissue culture."

chlorophyll – A molecule that plays a dominant role in the conversion of light energy into chemical energy during photosynthesis.

chlorosis – An absence of green pigments in plants due to lack of light or a magnesium or iron deficiency.

clone – The plants produced asexually from a single plant.

cultivar – A named plant variety under cultivation.

day length – The length of light period, either natural or artificial, given to plants to induce or prevent flowering.

disbud – The process of removing certain flower buds from the flowering stem to manipulate various characteristics of the flowering stem and flowers.

dormant – Resting or inactive growth.

flower – A blossom, usually colorful. A flower consists of the following parts:

calyx – the outer circle of sepals, usually green

corolla – the rings of petals, usually colorful

stamens – slender filaments tipped with anthers bearing pollen

pistil – the ovule-bearing and seed-bearing organ, often hidden in the center

foot candle – A standard measurement of the intensity of visible light. The light generated by a candle at a distance of one foot.

force – To bring into flower in advance of the normal blooming time.

fruit – Part of the plant that holds the seed.

genus – A subdivision of a plant family. The first word in a botanical name is the genus.

germination – The process seeds go through when they are changing from dormant states into newly sprouted seedlings.

growth regulators – Organic compounds that influence growth and multiplication.

growth retardant – Any chemical used to restrict the height of ornamental plants.

herb – A plant used for its scent, flavor, or medicinal value. Botanically, a plant lacking woody stem structure.

hormones – Natural or synthetic chemicals that strongly affect growth, such as cytokinins, auxins, and gibberellins.

humidity – The amount of water vapor in the air.

hybrid – A plant resulting from the crossing of two different plants of the same species, and differing markedly from either of its parents.

leach – To apply water or fertilizer solution in excess of what the soil can hold so that some portion of the applied liquid exits through the drain holes of pots.

leaf – The expanded organ, usually green, growing laterally from a stem. The parts of a leaf are:

blade - the broad expanded portion

petiole - the stem by which the blade is attached to the main stem or branch of the plant

stipule - a basal appendage, of which there are usually two, looking like small leaves, below the leaf stalk

loam – a fertile soil, either black or brown, coarser than clay, finer than sand, and containing organic matter.

medium – The material that plants are grown and anchored in.

micronutrients – The mineral fertilizer elements that are required by plants in very minute quantities.

perennial – A plant that does not die within a specified number of growing seasons, but maintains the capacity of grow anew each year from dormant tissue.

pH – A symbol of the degree of acidity or alkalinity, on a scale of 1 to 14.

photosynthesis – The process by which plants make carbohydrates from light and air.

pinch – To shorten stems by pinching out the bud or tip.

propagation – The process of producing new plants from the previous generation.

relative humidity – A measure of the amount of water present as vapor in the air.

salt index - Measurement of the amount of soluble salts a fertilier adds to the soil solution.

slip – A cutting.

soluble salts – The chemical salts or compounds that are dissolved in a solution. Soluble salts are contributed by the mineral salts naturally present in soils and irrigation water and by fertilizers and chemicals applied to the soil.

stock plants – Plants from which other plants are started.

sucker – A stem or shoot growing between the leaf and main stem.

tissue culture – Literally the culture of tissue. Propagation of new plants by nurturing one or more cells taken from a stock plant.

tuber – A short, fleshy, usually underground stem or shoot bearing minute leaves with buds in their axils. A tuber produces a new plant.

turgid – The condition of plant cells when they contain enough water to be in a normal expanded state.

vegetative - A plant in the non-sexually reproductive state.

vein – A sap-carrying vessel that forms the framework for the tissue of a leaf.

Index

CONVERSION LIST

SURFACE:

1 square inch = 6.5 square centimeters

1 square foot = 929 square centimeters
(0.0929 square meters)

1 square yard = 0.85 square meters

43,560 square feet = 1 acre

2.5 acres = 1 hectare = 10,000 square meters

1 quart per 100 sq. ft. = 100 gallons per acre

DRY WEIGHT:

1 ounce = 28.35 grams

1 pound = 454 grams = 16 ounces

1 pound of most fungicides per 100 gallons is equivalent to 1 tablespoon per gallon. (However, this equivalent can be off.)

1 tablespoon = 3 teaspoons

1 ounce active per 100 gallons = 75 ppm

1 ppm = 1 milligram per 100 grams or 0.001 ml. per liter

1 gram per 100 square feet = 1 pound per acre

LIQUID:

1 ounce = 29.6 ml. = 2 tablespoons

8 ounces = 1 cup; 2 cups = 1 pint

2 pints = 1 quart; 4 quarts = 1 gallon

10 liters = 2.64 gallons

1 gallon = 128 ounces = 3800 ml.
= 8.34 pounds of water

1 gallon of concentrate per 100 gallons of spray = 2½ tablespoons/gallon

1 quart per 100 gallons = ⅝ tablespoon per gallon

1 pint = 1 pound of water